THE EMPLOYMENT OF
CAMBRIDGE GRADUATES

T0382470

THE EMPLOYMENT OF
CAMBRIDGE GRADUATES

BY

CHRISTINE CRAIG

CAMBRIDGE
AT THE UNIVERSITY PRESS
1963

CAMBRIDGE UNIVERSITY PRESS
Cambridge, New York, Melbourne, Madrid, Cape Town,
Singapore, São Paulo, Delhi, Mexico City

Cambridge University Press
The Edinburgh Building, Cambridge CB2 8RU, UK

Published in the United States of America by Cambridge University Press, New York

www.cambridge.org
Information on this title: www.cambridge.org/9781107623798

First published 1963
Re-issued 2013

A catalogue record for this publication is available from the British Library

ISBN 978-1-107-62379-8 Paperback

FOREWORD

The University Appointments Boards exist to give advice and information about careers to Cambridge men and women and to act as a link between undergraduates and employers. It is therefore essential that the Boards' officers should know something of what has happened to students after they have started work in their various callings and professions.

In the period immediately preceding the Second World War the men's Board made plans for a 'follow-up' survey for this purpose. But before it could be carried out the war intervened and interrupted the careers of those who might have contributed relevant information. The original plans had to be drastically modified, but a different study was made which is embodied in the publication 'University Education and Business' issued in 1946.

In the post-war years the Boards were able to elicit piecemeal information from employers and from graduates about the progress of Cambridge recruits in many occupations. But the Boards felt that it would be desirable to arrange for a more systematic survey of what has actually happened to undergraduates who left the University some years ago. Hence the present survey. The Boards have not supervised the project in detail, but have given their approval to the general lines on which it has been conducted.

It cannot, of course, be assumed either that a survey of a different cross-section of under-graduates (i.e. those who left the University at times different from those covered by the survey) would necessarily show the same pattern or that the pattern of the past will necessarily be reproduced in the future. But the outcome of the survey should enable the Boards' officers—and indeed Tutors and other teaching officers who advise undergraduates—to assess new developments more effectively.

The aim of the survey was primarily to help the Appointments Boards in Cambridge If a study had been made of the careers followed by men and women of the same years in other Universities, the findings would not necessarily have been similar. But, if due allowances are made for this factor, the report will, we hope, be of wide interest both to those who educate young people of high intelligence and to those who may employ them.

On the Boards' behalf we should like to acknowledge most warmly the help which Mrs Craig, who was responsible for carrying out the survey, has received from numerous sources. The Department of Applied Economics (of which Mrs Craig was a member before undertaking this piece of work) has not only furnished expert advice, but provided facilities and secretarial assistance without which the work would have been greatly impeded. In particular, the Deputy Director, Mr John Utting, throughout contributed valuable suggestions and wise counsel. Mrs V. M. Drake acted as Mrs Craig's general assistant: and the tedious task of coding the replies to the questionnaires was meticulously discharged by Dr J. Jarvis and Miss Marcia Davies. The Editor of the *Financial Times* kindly gave advice on the method of presenting the pictorial diagrams.

They are also most grateful to Mr C. A. Harmer of Pye Ltd., and his colleagues for their help in giving a trial to the pilot questionnaire.

The Boards are also deeply indebted to International Computers and Tabulators Ltd., who undertook without a fee to put the data on punched cards and to carry out the necessary sorting and tabulating.

Finally, we must thank the University for providing a grant to meet the cost of the project: and, above all, the Cambridge men and women—more than three thousand of them—who have loyally co-operated with the survey by providing answers to satisfy our curiosity.

FRANK LEE
Chairman,
University of Cambridge
Appointments Board

M. L. CARTWRIGHT
Chairman,
University of Cambridge
Women's Appointments Board

CONTENTS

LIST OF TABLES AND DIAGRAMS

LIST OF TABLES AND DIAGRAMS

x

CHAPTER I

INTRODUCTION

1. The object

The object of the survey has been outlined by the Chairman of the Appointments Board's in the foreword to this report. The Board asked us to enquire into the present occupation of Cambridge graduates of 1952 and 1953, the levels of responsibility and the salaries they have attained, the satisfaction they derive from their occupations, and how they have progressed to their present positions. The Women's Appointments Board were also interested in the availability of married women graduates for work, in particular those who might be willing and able to return to work after a period occupied with domestic responsibilities. Questionnaires were sent out during July and August 1961, so that our information about the "present" relates mainly to the later part of 1961.

2. The sample

The Board had given careful thought to the question of the age of the graduates to be included in the survey. They wished them to have had sufficient time to become established in their work, to find out for themselves what was entailed by work in various fields, and to rectify if necessary any false starts. On the other hand they should be young enough to give the present generation of undergraduates some idea of what prospects lay ahead, in the not too distant future, in the various fields of work. Graduates of 1952 and 1953 seemed to be a good choice. Most of them would have done National Service either before or after graduation, but there would be few, if any, older men with war service. They would now mostly be in their early thirties, and would have started work long enough after the end of the war for conditions of employment to be fairly normal. Many of them would have had 8 or 9 years at work; long enough to become established in their careers, but not too long to remember the main events of their working lives.

The women graduates chosen were those of the same two years and also those of 1937 and 1938. The latter were included with the particular object of investigating the position of married women in their forties who might be available for work after the most pressing demands of young children were relaxed. In both groups, graduates of two successive years were chosen in order to obtain a reasonably large sample, fairly homogeneous in respect of age.

Completed questionnaires were received from 2630 men and 494 women. This represents 70% of all the men and 80% of all the women graduates on the College lists for the appropriate years; it is 83% and 90% respectively of those whose addresses we could trace. (Up-to-date addresses were not available for a number of graduates.) The questionnaire, response, and the reliability of the information are discussed in some detail in Appendix I.

3. Presentation of the results

The members of the sample have one characteristic in common; they are all Cambridge graduates. Otherwise there are fundamental differences in the sample which are relevant to the kind of work they were doing, and which have determined the way in which we have presented the results of the enquiry. These are sex, country of origin and place of work. 84 of the women, mainly nationals of the United Kingdom, were married, and living overseas by virtue of their husband's jobs. There were 434 men living overseas; the majority of these were British nationals, but they included 85 Commonwealth and foreign nationals who came to the United Kingdom for their University education and then returned to their own countries to work.

Nothing is said in Chapter II about the 85 men of Commonwealth and foreign nationality who have returned to their country of origin. These were excluded because their general background was so different from that of the United Kingdom nationals and could not be discussed in the same terms. On the other hand, they were too heterogeneous a group to be considered separately.

At the beginning of Chapters III and IV, the current employment status of the women and their overall earnings are given in order to show how they compare with the men. The rest of the material reviewing the experience of the women after leaving Cambridge has, however, been presented separately in Chapter VII. The two questionnaires did not cover quite the same ground, and much of the information we asked for from the women did not apply to the men.

Most of the results given for the men relate to those working in the United Kingdom at the time of the survey. The men working outside the United Kingdom had been overseas for very varying lengths of time, employed in a variety of ways, and it was not always possible to distinguish those who were permanently overseas from those who intended to return to the United Kingdom at some time in the future, nor those employed by firms or organisations in the United Kingdom from those in professions or businesses with no direct connection with the United Kingdom. We therefore decided to present the information relating to the men in the United Kingdom independently, and outline in a separate chapter the main differences in overseas working conditions.

The following summary shows which graduates are discussed in each chapter.

Chapter II.   The graduates' background. All women and men except the 85 men of Commonwealth and foreign nationality who have returned to their country of origin.

Chapter III.   Current employment. The general position is shown for both men and women graduates. The employment of the men working in the United Kingdom is then discussed in some detail.

Chapter IV.   Earnings and satisfaction of men working in the United Kingdom. Earnings of women working full-time in the United Kingdom are also shown for comparison, but are given in more detail in Chapter VII.

Chapter V.   The past and the future. Men working in the United Kingdom. First appointments, changes of employer, and expectations for the future.

Chapter VI.   Men working overseas. A brief review of the kind of employment and of earnings.

Chapter VII.   The women graduates. Current employment position and the availability for work of those not working in paid employment at the time of the survey.

Chapter VIII. Summary.

4. Some definitions

Career is used as a convenient term to describe a way of making a livelihood, not necessarily progress up a particular ladder or within a particular occupation.

Progress is used to describe a succession of events in the graduate's working life, and does not necessarily imply a series of stages of promotion.

Several men objected to both these terms, on the grounds that they implied an assumption that all men had, or should have, a specific occupation with recognisable stages of promotion. We wish to emphasise that we make no such assumption.

Unemployed is used to describe those not working in *paid* employment. Some of the 'unemployed' men were engaged in full-time study, and most of the 'unemployed' women were fully occupied with domestic and voluntary work.

Employment group. This refers to the employer, or the business or practice in which the graduate was working, and the heading does not always indicate the type of work. For example, a lawyer working in a private solicitor's practice as a partner or a salaried employee is classified under the heading 'Private legal practice'; a solicitor working as a legal advisor to a manufacturing company is classified under 'Industry', and one employed as town clerk to a local authority is classified under 'Local government'. (Table 15 in Chapter III shows the type of work within the various employment groups for all United Kingdom men.)

The employment groups are based on the Standard Industrial Classification (Central Statistical Office, 1958) with slight modifications in the grouping of individual types of employment under main headings. The content of the groups used in this report is as follows:

Agriculture
Farming, estate management, forestry and horticulture.

Industry
- (a) Mining and quarrying
- (b) Manufacturing industry
- (c) Construction, including civil engineering contractors
- (d) Public utilities (gas, electricity and water)
- (e) Transport and communications

Commerce
- (a) Distributive trades
- (b) Insurance, banking and finance

Private professional practices
- (a) Accountancy
- (b) Law (barristers and solicitors)
- (c) Other private practices and services
    - (i) Civil and other engineering consultants
    - (ii) Architects
    - (iii) Estate agents and surveyors
    - (iv) Advertising agents
    - (v) Management consultants
    - (vi) Other

Medicine

    (*a*) General practice; private and National Health Service

    (*b*) Hospitals, hospital boards and management committees

Education

    (*a*) Schools

    (*b*) Universities, technical colleges and institutes, teacher training colleges, theological colleges

Research establishments

    (*a*) Industrial research associations and independent establishments whose activities are mainly or wholly research and development. Research and planning departments which form part of manufacturing concerns are classified under 'Industry'.

    (*b*) Government and Government sponsored research establishments and institutes. These include units administered by the D.S.I.R., the Medical Research Council, and the Agricultural Research Council

    (*c*) The United Kingdom Atomic Energy Authority

Government service

    (*a*) The Civil Service. All members of the administrative civil service and the Foreign Service. Technical, professional, scientific and specialist civil servants, other than those classified under Government research institutes

    (*b*) Local government. All local authority posts other than those in schools and further education.

Journalism, arts and entertainment

    Newspapers and publishers (free-lance journalists and authors are included), theatre, films, radio, television, musicians and artists, etc.

The Church

    Ministers of religion of all denominations, excluding those employed in, and classified under, schools, universities or one of the armed forces

The Forces

    All members of the Royal Navy, Royal Air Force and the Army, including chaplains and doctors. National Servicemen are included.

Miscellaneous

    All types of employment not elsewhere specified; including catering, trade associations and business services, political organisations, welfare and charitable organisations, and the head offices of enterprises operating abroad.

Earnings. We use the term 'basic earnings' to refer to annual salary or earnings excluding the value of any allowances or fringe benefits, and 'total earnings' to refer to salary plus the value of any additional emoluments. These are explained in more detail in Chapter IV.

Median and quartile earnings. When the earnings of a group of people are listed in order of magnitude, the median is the middle value, with as many above as below. It is unaffected by extreme values at either end of the distribution, whereas the arithmetic average may be considerably affected by a few extreme values. In this group of Cambridge graduates some occupation groups contained a small number of people earning very much more than the rest, so that the median values are generally more typical than the averages. The lower quartile is a figure of annual earnings such that one-quarter of the group earn less than this amount; the upper quartile gives the figure which is exceeded by one-quarter. The differences between the lower and the upper quartiles (the inter-quartile range) shows the range of earnings of the central half of the group.

We review the graduates' current earnings in Chapter IV, where we give tables showing the average, median and quartile earnings in various groups. We use this form of presentation as a convenient summary of the central tendency and spread of earnings in each group. Distribution tables are also used to give greater detail of the whole range. Figures for average, median and quartile earnings should be treated with caution when dealing with very small groups, when a few atypical figures may considerably affect the results, and it is in any case difficult to decide what is 'typical'. No average or median values have been calculated for less than 20 graduates.

5. The tables

The number of graduates answering each question was not always the same, so that the totals may differ from table to table. When the figures are given in percentages, these are usually percentages of the known total, i.e. of the number of graduates answering that question. In cases where we have included the unknown values in the total, these are shown in the tables. The percentages have been rounded to the nearest whole number, and significance should not be attached to small percentage differences, particularly in small groups. A group which contains some graduates, but less than 1% of the total, is indicated by the symbol ø.

CHAPTER II

THE GRADUATES' BACKGROUND

It is perhaps obvious that no survey of this kind can show how far people and events are influenced by differences in personality and temperament, but it is worth emphasising that these intangible factors are sometimes as important in determining the course of a graduate's career as his qualifications. It is, however, largely his educational background and academic qualifications that determine which fields of employment are open to him. This chapter reviews the graduates' background and qualifications; subsequent chapters compare progress and opportunities in various fields.

The data given in this chapter refers to all the graduates except the 85 men of foreign and Commonwealth nationality who returned to their country of origin after completing their studies. The other graduates now resident overseas are included here, since for most of them the decision to leave the United Kingdom was taken after they had finished their education.

1. The general background

Most of the 1952/53 graduates were born between 1928 and 1932, and much of their time at school was during the Second World War. They left school between 1945 and 1950,

TABLE 1. *Age Distribution*

(Percentage of each group)

	1952/1953		1937/1938	
Age	Men	Women	Age	Women
27–29	6	18		
30	16	44	44	12
31	28	28	45	38
32	30	4	46	32
33	14	3	47	15
34–39	5	2	48 and over	3
40 and over	1	1		
Total percentage	100	100		100
Total number of graduates	2630	284		210

just after the Education Acts of 1944 and 1945, and came up to Cambridge in 1949 and 1950. The men were liable for National Service, which most of them did before coming up, although a number were deferred until after graduation. A small number of older men had some war service, and came up to Cambridge when they were in their thirties.

Most of the 1937/38 women graduates were born during the First World War, between 1914 and 1917; they left school in the early thirties and came up to Cambridge in 1934 and 1935, graduating a year or two before the outbreak of the Second World War. Many of them therefore spent their early working years in war-time conditions.

At the time of the survey 94% of the 1952/53 graduates were aged between 29 and 33. There were 89 men over 35, most of whom had either taken a degree at another University or been in the Forces before coming up to Cambridge. The women graduates of 1952/53 had a slightly lower average age than the men, since most of them had come direct from school to university, whereas the majority of the men had gone from school to National Service. Most of the 1937/38 women graduates were in their forties at the time of the survey.

2. Home background

Home background is indicated in very general terms by grouping father's occupation into Social Class Categories.* These are very broad groups, whose main value in this context is in distinguishing Social Class I (occupations requiring professional qualifications) and Social Class III or below (manual and lower grade non-manual occupations). Social Class II covers a very wide range of mainly non-manual occupations, appropriately described as 'Intermediate', and would include most of the people who might describe themselves as middle middle class. Members of the Armed Forces are excluded from this classification and are shown separately in Table 2.

TABLE 2. *Father's Occupation*

(Percentage of each group)

		1952/1953		1937/1938
	Social Class Category	Men	Women	Women
I	Professionally qualified	28	28	42
	Armed Forces: Commissioned ranks	5	5	4
II	Intermediate: Managerial, executive, higher grade non-manual	50	52	45
III	Skilled manual and lower grade non-manual	14	14	8
IV & V	Semi-skilled and unskilled manual	2	1	1
	Not known	1	—	—
	Total percentage	100	100	100
	Total number of graduates	2545	284	210

This shows the predominance of the middle classes, with over a quarter of all the graduates of both sexes from homes in the professionally qualified classes, less than a fifth from Social Class III or below. More of the pre-war graduates came from the professional classes, under a tenth from Social Class III and IV.

3. Type of school

Two-thirds of the men came from independent schools. These have not been further categorised, but almost all were independent schools belonging to the Head Masters' Conference. It is interesting to compare the lower proportion of women from independent

* General Register Office, Classification of Occupations 1960. H.M.S.O.

schools in both age groups. There is probably more than one reason for this difference. One might be the view, common in many families, that a 'good' education is less of a necessity for girls than boys, and if there is a choice between the children, the boys should be given priority. This would result in fewer of the potential women undergraduates going to a public school in the first place. It is also probable that girls at public schools used to

TABLE 3. *Type of Secondary School*

| | 1952/1953 | | | | 1937/1938 | |
| | Men | | Women | | Women | |
	Number	Per cent	Number	Per cent	Number	Per cent
Independent school	1557	61	119	42	112	54
Direct grant grammar school	298	12	49	18	47	22
L.E.A. grammar school	597	24	91	32	42	20
Foreign school	39	1	12	4	9	4
Not known	54	2	13	4	—	—
Total	2545	100	284	100	210	100

be less university minded than their brothers, fewer of them thinking of a university education as an essential preliminary to a career. The legend of the unfeminine university bluestocking dies hard, and is perhaps still not entirely dead.

After leaving school most of the women went straight to university, but nearly three-quarters of the men had a gap of over a year.

TABLE 4. *Time between leaving School and coming up to Cambridge: Men*

	Number	Per cent
Under 3 months	431	17
3 months–1 year	258	10
Over 1 year up to 2 years	1346	53
Over 2 years up to 3 years	337	13
Over 3 years	157	6
Not known	16	1
Total	2545	100

The majority—66%—spent the time in National Service, and a few (63 men) had 3 or more years in National Service or War Service. 60 men had spent 2 or more years at another university, 73 did shorter periods of study, mostly working for scholarship examinations. 250 spent some time in paid employment, mostly for a year or less, but a few for a longer period.

4. National Service

We were interested to see if the men felt that the time they spent in National Service had had any bearing on their subsequent careers. There was no evidence that it made any difference to their choice of subject when they came up to Cambridge. Excluding those who intended to study medicine, 32% of the National Servicemen read engineering, science or mathematics, and 68% other subjects, as against 33% and 67% of those who had a time gap not due to National Service, and 34% and 66% of those who went straight to Cambridge from school. Those who came up to read medicine (194 men) had nearly all made their choice before or shortly after leaving school, and less than a third of them did National Service before coming to Cambridge.

TABLE 5. *Scholarships and other Awards*

(Percentage of each group)

| | 1952/1953 | | 1937/1938 |
	Men	Women	Women
School open scholarship	3	1	5
College entrance open scholarship	18	14	20
State scholarship	6	20	8
State plus college entrance scholarship	7	7	10
Other open university scholarship	1	1	1
Closed scholarships (school and university)	3	2	6
L.E.A. award	18	27	3
F.E.T.S. award	12	—	—
Other awards	4	2	2
No award	28	22	45
Not known	—	4	—
Total percentage	100	100	100
Total number of graduates	2545	284	210

Question 10 asked the men to say what they did in any gap between leaving school and coming up to Cambridge, and then asked 'What, if any, bearing did this have on your subsequent career?' In answering this question, most of the National Servicemen said that their time in the Forces had no direct bearing on their subsequent choice of career. There were a few who said that their experience made them resolve not to go into the Forces after graduation and also a small number who were sufficiently attracted by Service life to return to the Forces after graduation, or, in the case of a few whose National Service was deferred until after graduation, to transfer to a short service or permanent commission. Many felt, however, that their service had matured them and made them more able to benefit from university life, and given them experience of mixing with different kinds of people which was valuable later on. On the other hand there were also quite a number who felt they suffered a set-back through the break in their studies, and found university work harder in consequence.

5. Scholarships and awards

About three-quarters of the 1952/53 graduates, both men and women, came up to Cambridge with some kind of scholarship or grant, but only just over half the 1937/38 women, the difference being due to the smaller number of State and L.E.A. awards given before the war. The main types of award are shown below (Table 5). Several graduates had more than one award; those who gained both a state and an open college or university scholarship are shown separately in Table 5; in other cases only one award has been recorded, open scholarships being coded in preference to closed scholarships, L.E.A. grants or grants given under the 'Further Education and Training Scheme' for ex-Servicemen.

TABLE 6. *Scholarships and other Awards, by Type of School: Men*

(Percentage in each type of school)

School	All open and State scholarships	All closed scholarships	L.E.A. awards	F.E.T.S. awards	Other awards	No award	Total
Independent	29	3	14	11	3	40	100
Direct grant	54	3	25	9	3	6	100
L.E.A.	53	1	29	7	4	6	100

A higher proportion of boys from non-independent schools gained scholarships. This is not unexpected, since most of the grammar school boys would not have been able to afford to come to Cambridge without an award of some sort.

Looking ahead to the Cambridge degree examinations, there is also evidence that more graduates from non-independent schools reached a higher academic standard.

TABLE 7. *Class of Degree by Type of School: Men*

(Percentage in each type of school)

School	Degree Class				Total
	1st	2nd	3rd	Ordinary	
Independent	7	55	31	7	100
Direct grant	11	67	21	1	100
L.E.A.	12	66	18	4	100

6. University subjects

Rather more than half the men read for an arts degree, about a third for a degree in science or mathematics, and the remainder for a degree in engineering, agriculture, estate management or architecture. A rather higher proportion of the women read arts subjects, and very few read engineering, agriculture, estate management or architecture.

This gives the general picture, but there are differences within the subjects shown in Table 8 which need some explanation. First, there are differences in the level of specialisation in the science, mathematics and engineering subjects. For example, science includes three groups, (*a*) those who spent three years on part I of the natural sciences tripos, (*b*) those who passed part I in two years and spent a third year on a different subject, and (*c*) the more specialised scientists who passed part I in two years and went on to specialise in one branch of science in part II in their third year. The scientists also include those who read natural sciences and were awarded a B.A. before going on to qualify in medicine (7% of the men, 6–8% of the women. Most of these read part I, but a few passed part II examinations also).

The greater number of mathematicians were those who passed part II of the mathematics tripos in their third year, having previously passed part I. The more specialised mathematicians read for part II of the tripos in their second or third years and then went on to part III in their third or fourth years.

'Engineering' includes (a) those who took the engineering studies course, which leads to an Ordinary degree; (b) those who spent three years on part I of the mechanical sciences tripos; and the more specialised engineers who either (c) passed part I of the mechanical sciences tripos in two years and part II in their third year, or (d) passed the chemical engineering tripos in their third or fourth year after first reading one of the less specialised engineering or science subjects.

TABLE 8. *Degree Subject: Arts v. Science and Technology*

(Percentage of each group)

	1952/1953		1937/1938
Subject	Men	Women	Women
Engineering	11	1	—
Science and mathematics	31	37	37
Agriculture, estate management, architecture	5	1	1
Arts	53	61	62
Total percentage	100	100	100
Total number of graduates	2545	284	210

Secondly, there are a number of combinations of different subjects for which a degree may be awarded, and nearly a quarter (23%) of the men changed subjects during their time at Cambridge. This flexibility in the system of awarding degrees has obvious advantages for the undergraduate, who does not have to commit himself to a particular course of study from the beginning of his university career; he may start with the intention of reading more than one subject, or change horses in midstream if he regrets his original choice. In cases where there were changes, we have used some fairly arbitrary rules for classifying the 'Main' subject (see Appendix II). There were few changes between the arts and science or engineering; the most common changes were between science and engineering subjects, or between arts subjects.

These variations are not very important when considering overall differences between subjects, but when discussing particular subjects it should be remembered that we are sometimes generalising about graduates who have qualified in rather different ways. Degree subject distribution is given in some detail in Appendix II, with a note indicating which were the most common combinations of subject.

7. Class of degree

Degree class was coded as the class awarded for the final examination before graduating, or if there was a change of subjects the class obtained in what was regarded as the main subject. The table below shows the distribution of the five Honours classes, with all Ordinary degrees as a sixth single group. The courses in agriculture, estate management and architecture, which at that time led only to an Ordinary degree, have been treated as Honours courses.

The men's attainments seem broadly to be inferior to the women's, with a lower proportion of upper Second Class Honours, and a higher proportion of Third Class Honours and Ordinary degrees. 2·5% of the men (64 graduates) read engineering studies or Christian theology, both courses leading to an Ordinary degree, i.e. an Honours class was not a

TABLE 9. *Degree Class*

(percentage of each group)

	1952/1953		1937/1398
Class	Men	Women	Women
I	9	7	13
2.i	19	30	27
2.ii	30	40	20
2 undivided	10	3	18
3	26	18	20
Ordinary	6	2	2
Total percentage	100	100	100
Total number of graduates	2545	284	210

possibility in these cases. No women took these courses, so their chances of obtaining an Honours degree were slightly greater. Nevertheless, this factor is not so important as to affect significantly the overall comparison of Honours classes.

Differences of class between subjects is obscured to some extent by the practice of awarding undivided Second Class Honours for mathematics and some engineering examinations, so that direct comparison is only possible between First and Third Class Honours and Ordinary degrees. The class distribution within engineering, mathematics, science and arts suggests that scientists and mathematicians tended to get more First Class Honours and fewer Ordinary degrees than the arts graduates, but that the arts graduates gained in the intermediate classes, having fewer thirds and more seconds (see Table 10). In other words, there appeared to be more very good mathematics and science graduates, but the less good tended to be more mediocre than the arts men. Engineering graduates seemed to do less well than either, having fewer firsts, and more thirds and Ordinary degrees. There are, however, clear differences within the non-arts subjects, due to the different levels of specialisation already mentioned. The engineers, mathematicians and scientists who took the higher tripos examinations had a better academic record than either graduates in the same subjects or the arts graduates. This is to be expected, since they would have to be among the best graduates in these subjects, academically speaking, to be able to read for the higher tripos examinations.

TABLE 10. *Degree Class by Subject: Men*

(percentage of each subject)

Subject	Class				Total	Number
	1	All 2	3	Ordinary		
Engineering studies	—	—	—	100	100	42
Mechanical sciences I	5	35	53	7	100	165
Mechanical sciences II[1]	9	91	—	—	100	56
Chemical engineering	8	46	33	13	100	24
All engineering	6	43	31	20	100	287
Mathematics II	8	39	47	6	100	97
Mathematics III[1]	39	61	—	—	100	53
All mathematics	19	46	31	4	100	150
Natural sciences I	3	57	38	2	100	315
Natural sciences II	17	61	21	1	100	309
All science	10	59	30	1	100	624
Economics	4	69	25	2	100	77
Law	5	52	34	9	100	333
Other arts	8	69	17	6	100	942

1. For Mechanical Sciences part II, and Mathematics part III, candidates are awarded Honours or Honours with distinction. These have been recorded as an undivided class 2, and first class respectively. This is in line with the graduates' achievements in their earlier examinations (Mechanical Sciences I and Mathematics II).

8. Further qualifications

For many graduates their B.A. is only the first stage in becoming qualified for a specific profession, such as medicine, law, accountancy or architecture, and many others obtain additional qualifications which also require further study and examinations. These various additional qualifications are very much part of the graduate's background, which have to be taken into account when comparing their experience in various fields of work.

66% of the men had some additional qualification, 60% of the younger women, and 56% of the older women. Table 11 shows what the main qualifications were.

For both groups of women the most common additional qualification was the post-graduate Diploma of Education, taken by a fifth of the women as against a tenth of the men. The proportions who qualified in medicine (8–9%) and for a Ph.D. (4–8%) were similar for men and the younger women, rather lower among the women who graduated before the war, when doctorates were less common. Only four women had additional legal qualifications and no women qualified for other professional practices. In contrast, over a quarter of the men obtained qualifications for the various professions, including medicine and the Church, and 5% of the men qualified for membership of the various engineering institutes, with no competition from the women.

TABLE 11. *Additional Qualifications*

(percentage of each group)

Qualification	1952/1953		1937/1938
	Men	Women	Women
Other first degree	2	4	4
Qualifications essential or usual for practice			
Medical	9	8	9
Legal	7	1	—
Chartered accountants and actuaries	3	—	—
Architecture	1	—	—
Estate management and surveyors	1	—	—
Church ordination	5	—	—
Membership of engineering Institutions			
Civil engineers	2	—	—
Other engineers	3	—	—
Diploma or Certificate of Education	10	20	21
Post-graduate diplomas and higher degrees normally requiring			
1 year of study[1]	2	6	7
2 years of study	2	4	2
3 years of study (Ph.D.)	7	8	4
Miscellaneous qualifications[2]	11	9	8
No additional qualification	35	40	45
Total percentage	100	100	100
Total number of graduates	2545	284	210

1. Other than Diploma of Education and Church Ordination.
2. The miscellaneous qualifications cover a very wide range; they are mainly memberships of various professional and learned societies and institutes, some gained by examination, others not. A full-time course of study is not normally essential.

9. Marriage

To complete this outline of the graduates' background, their marital status at the time of the survey is shown below:

TABLE 12. *Marital Status*, 1961

(percentage of each group)

	1952/1953		1937/1938
	Men	Women	Women
Single	27	27	30
Married with no children	14	14	5
Married with 1 or 2 children	47	41	20
Married with 3 or more children	11	17	38
Widowed and divorced	1	1	7
Total percentage	100	100	100
Total number of graduates	2545	284	210

The marriage rate among the graduates was evidently rather different from that of comparable age groups of the general population, with a markedly higher proportion of single women in the graduate group, and even among the men, a rather higher proportion of bachelors than among the general population.* The women tended to marry earlier than the men. Taking the graduates of 1952/1953 who were married at the time of the survey, we find that within the first year after graduation 25% of the women and 19% of the men were married; by the third year 59% of the women and 49% of the men; by the sixth year 87% of the former and 84% of the latter.

	England and Wales: Percentage of population 1960		*Cambridge graduates: Percentage of 1961 sample*	
			Graduates of 1952/1953	
(a) Age 25–34:	Men	Women	Men	Women
Single	22	12	26	27
Married	77	87	73	72
Widowed	1	1	1	1
			Graduates of 1937/1938:	
(b) Age 40–49:		Women		Women
Single		10		30
Married		85		63
Widowed		5		7

* Comparative figures of marital status for the population of England and Wales as a whole are as follows (Registrar General's Stat. Rev. for 1960):

CHAPTER III

CURRENT EMPLOYMENT

1. The graduates in general

At the time of the survey 87% of the men were working as salaried employees, and 12% were working on their own account or as partners in private companies or practices. (See table 13.) 1% were working only part-time or were temporarily unemployed, including 6 men engaged in full-time study. Doctors in the National Health Service working as principals or partners in general practice have been included with the self-employed.

TABLE 13. *Current Employment Status*

| | 1952/1953 | | | | 1937/1938 | |
| | Men | | Women | | Women | |
	U.K.	Overseas	U.K.	Overseas	U.K.	Overseas
Full-time work:						
Self-employed	290	34	2	—	1	1
Employed in family business	73	14	—	—	—	—
Other employed	1812	380	78	23	79	8
Part-time work:						
Self-employed	2	—	12	2	6	1
Employed	6	—	25	6	35	—
Unemployed	13	6	110	26	62	17
Total	2196	434	227	57	183	27

Both the salaried employees and the self-employed include a number of men working in a family business or practice. We did not ask a specific question about this, and although a number of men volunteered the information, it is impossible to say what the total number is. The mobility, earnings and prospects of those known to be in a family business were often rather different from the rest of the group, and in order to illustrate the differences some of the results have been analysed separately for the 73 men in the United Kingdom know to be employed in a family business. No separate analyses of this kind have been made for self-employed men, because there were too few known cases to make it worthwhile. None of the women admitted to working in a family business, and there were in any case rather few women working in private concerns.

49% of the 1952/1953 women and 38% of the 1937/1938 women graduates were not working in paid employment at the time of the survey; all but a few of these were married with children. The majority of the women working full-time in both age groups were not married.

2. Type of employment

The overseas men were slightly differently distributed from those in the United Kingdom with a higher proportion in civilian government service, universities and colleges of further education, and a lower proportion in schools and professional practices. The outstanding difference between the men and women was the very much higher proportion of women in education and the relatively small number in all other fields except medicine and government service. Table 14 shows the differences in the main fields of employment. There is no doubt that many women go into the educational field from choice, but comments on the women's questionnaires make it clear that a number of this group did so because of the lack of suitable openings elsewhere, and the feeling that prejudice against women in

TABLE 14. *Comparative Distribution of some of the main Employment Groups*

(percentage of each group)

	1952/1953			1937/1938
	Men		Women United Kingdom and overseas	Women United Kingdom and overseas
	Overseas	United Kingdom		
Industry and commerce	33	32	6	1
Medicine	5	8	11	8
Other professional practices	6	12	2	5
Schools	7	15	24	44
Universities, technical training colleges	14	9	21	15
Civilian government service and U.K.A.E.A.	18	9	10	11
Other	17	15	26	16
Total percentage	100	100	100	100
Total number of graduates	428	2183	148	131

industry and commerce and the professions, other than medicine, made them unable to compete against men in these fields.

3. Men working in the United Kingdom

Table 15 shows, under the main employment group headings, where the men in the United Kingdom were working at the time of the survey. (The employment groups are defined in Chapter I.) Table 16 shows the type of work within the main employment groups.

A third of all the men were working in industry or commerce, a quarter were in education of some kind, and a fifth were in either medicine, law or other professional practices; 8% were in civilian government service (including those in the United Kingdom Atomic Energy Authority), 6% in the Church, and between 2% and 3% in each of the groups included under the Forces, agriculture, and journalism, art and entertainment. The largest groups of self-employed men were in law, agriculture, and commerce. The men known to be employed in family firms were almost all in industry and commerce.

TABLE 15. *Distribution by Employment Group and Employment Status: Men working in the United Kingdom*

Employment group	Employed		Self-employed		Employed in family business		All United Kingdom men	
	Number	%	Number	%	Number	%	Number	%
Agriculture	10	1	45	15	3	4	58	3
Manufacturing industry and mining	419		5		45		469	
Construction	16		3		—		19	
Public utilities	5		—		—		5	
Transport and communications	18		3		1		22	
Industry	458	25	11	4	46	63	515	24
Distributive trades	50		10		13		73	
Insurance, banking and finance	82		20		5		107	
Commerce	132	7	30	10	18	25	180	8
Accountancy	13		12		—		25	
Law	37		88		1		126	
Medicine	119		56		—		175	
Other professional practices	86		26		—		112	
Professional practices	255	14	182	63	1	1	438	20
Church	121	7	—	—	—	—	121	6
Industrial research establishments	35		—	—	—	—	35	
Government research institutes	29		—	—	—	—	29	
U.K.A.E.A.	29		—	—	—	—	29	
Research establishments	93	5	—	—	—	—	93	4
Schools	328	18	5	—	1	—	334	15
Universities, technical and training colleges	188	10	—	—	—	—	188	9
Civil service	74		—	—	—	—	74	
Local government	33		—	—	—	—	33	
Government services	107	6	—	—	—	—	107	5
Forces	50	3					50	2
National Service	5						5	0
Journalism, art and entertainment	29	1	17	6	2	3	48	2
Miscellaneous	44	2	—	—	2	3	46	2
All United Kingdom men { Percentage		100		100		100		100
All United Kingdom men { Number	1820		290		73		2183	

Industry was the largest single employment group, with 25% of all the graduates, including those working in industrial research establishments. Within this group, the type of work classified under research, design, development and planning was the most common (Table 15—31% of the men in industry come under this heading). This covers a fairly wide field of activities, and includes 'pure' scientific research; plant, instrument and

TABLE 16. *Type of Work by Employment Group: Men working in the United Kingdom*[1]

Type of work	Employment group								Total	
	Industry[2]	Commerce including distributive trades	Civil[3] service and U.K.A.E.A.	Local government	Forces	Professional practices	Arts and entertainment	Other[4]	Number of men	Percentage of all men
General administration and management	82	48	30	—	9	—	5	22	196	9
Production, operation and maintenance[5]	96	—	4	3	17	—	1	1	122	6
Accounting, banking, insurance and finance	21	75[6]	12[7]	1	—	28	—	3	140	6
Sales, advertising, market research	128	31	1	—	—	25	1	1	187	9
Research, design, development	172	10	61	1	9	2	2	11	268	13
Information, advisory, consultant	20	2	9	3	—	48[9]	—	19	101	5
Writing, editing, publishing, producing	—	—	—	—	—	—	39[11]	2	41	2
Teaching	—	—	—	—	5	—	—	495	500	23
Architecture, estate agency and surveying	2	8	3	6	—	31	—	—	50	2
Medical	1	—	2	1	12[8]	175	—	—	191	8
Legal and patent	7	2	6	16	—	129[10]	—	1	161	7
Church, pastoral	—	1	—	—	3	—	—	125	128	6
Farming and estate management; forestry	—	—	2	—	—	—	—	58	61	3
Personnel and social work	16	3	2	2	—	—	—	3	26	1
Miscellaneous	5	—	—	—	—	—	—	—	5	—
Total	550	180	132	33	55	438	48	741	2177	100

1. Type of work not known for 6 men. 2. Including industrial research establishments. 3. Including government research institutes. 4. Schools, universities, churches, agriculture and miscellaneous—i.e. those groups where the type of work is almost all of one kind, and is fairly obvious from the employment group. 5. Includes maintenance engineers in the civil service, local government, the Forces and radio. 6. 8 qualified accountants and actuaries; 15 others in general banking; 30 in insurance; 22 in stockbroking and finance. 7. 11 inspectors of taxes. 8. 5 doctors doing National Service. 9. 23 civil engineers, 12 other engineering consultants, 14 management consultants. 10. 35 barristers; 94 solicitors. 11. 23 men in journalism, writing, editing and publishing; 16 in radio, T.V., film, theatre and music.

structural design and development; the development of a variety of manufactured products; design and planning of processes and control systems; and economic, financial and mathematical research and planning of all kinds. The men working in industrial research establishments, as distinct from those in the planning and research departments of factories, tended to be engaged in more fundamental research, whereas those in the research and planning departments were more often doing development and design work with a direct bearing on the work of the production departments. There was, in fact, sometimes considerable overlap between the work in production and planning departments, and it should be noted that the classifications shown in Table 16 are not entirely clear-cut; they describe the type of work in which the graduate appeared to spend most, but not necessarily all, of his time.

TABLE 17. *Research, Design, Development and Planning: Men working in the United Kingdom*

	In industry and industrial research establishments	Other than industry
Civil engineering	7	—
Other engineering	74	11
Statistics, economics and computing	37	19
Physical and chemical sciences	35	26
Biological sciences	11	35
Other and not known	8	4
Total	172	95

The majority of the men engaged in research, development and planning in industry were doing work in engineering or one of the physical sciences; a higher proportion of those outside industry were doing research in medicine and the biological sciences, mainly in the scientific Civil Service, including Government research institutes.

A further 23% of the men in industry were in sales, marketing and market research; a more detailed breakdown of their functions is shown in Table 18. Outside industry almost all those doing sales and advertising work were in commerce or advertising agencies.

Another 17% of the men in industry were concerned with production, operation and maintenance, and 15% were doing general management work. The general administration and management group contains rather a variety of jobs at different levels of responsibility, ranging from general managers of industrial establishments to personal assistants to the general managers. It was not practicable, however, to attempt any 'grading' of these jobs; the variations between different firms and in the graduates' descriptions of their jobs make comparisons very difficult, if not meaningless.

Commerce. A third of the men in commerce were self-employed or employed in a family firm. Most of the latter were in the distributive trades; the self-employed were running retail businesses, or were partners in stockbroking, property and finance firms. Most of the other salaried employees in commerce were fairly evenly divided among the distributive trades, insurance companies and banking.

Education. Teaching of various kinds was the most common occupation, and more men were employed in schools than in any other group except industry. 113 men were teaching in independent secondary schools, 171 in L.E.A. or direct grant grammar schools, and 34 in preparatory schools. (16 did not give the type of school.) In view of the current shortage of science teachers, it was somewhat discouraging to find that three-quarters were teaching arts subjects, and only a quarter were teaching science or mathematics.

The men teaching in universities, technical colleges, teacher's and theological colleges are shown together in Table 15. The majority of these were in universities (8% of all the men as against 1%—or 35 men—in the other establishments). Here, rather more than half (57%) were teaching engineering, science or mathematics, and less than half (42%) were teaching arts subjects.

Private professional practices. 12% of the men were in private professional practices other than medicine, half of these in law (i.e. 6% of all the men), the greatest number as

TABLE 18. *Sales, Marketing and Advertising: Men working in the United Kingdom*

	Industry	Commerce	Private practices
General sales work	39	15	—
Technical sales work	25	1	—
Representatives	10	6	—
Buyers	10	4	—
Marketing and market research	39	5	3
Advertising	5	—	22
Total	128	31	25

principals or partners in firms of solicitors. The other private professional practices included accountancy, firms of engineering consultants, management consultants, architects, surveyors, estate agents and advertising agents.

Medicine. 8% of the men were practising medicine. Those shown as self-employed in Table 15 were principals or partners in general practice, almost all under the National Health Service. Most of the employed doctors were in hospital posts, as house physicians, surgeons or registrars. A small number were employed as assistants in general practice. This group also includes the 4 men who were dentists or veterinary surgeons.

Civilian Government Service. 5% of the men were in the Civil Service, and 2% in local government posts. The civil servants included 30 men in administrative grades and 32 in the Scientific Civil Service (this includes those in government research institutes, but not the 29 men doing research work in the U.K.A.E.A.). There were also small numbers of men in various specialist and technical posts, as tax inspectors, engineers, legal advisers, architects, doctors and forestry advisors.

Half the men in local government posts were qualified solicitors working as town clerks. The remainder included engineers, architects and librarians.

The Armed Forces. There were 5 doctors completing their National Service, all of whom were shortly returning to civilian life. 50 were regular officers; 26 in the Navy, 16 in the

Army, and 8 in the Air Force. 32 out of the 50 men in the regular Forces had been commissioned before coming up to Cambridge, and had therefore returned to their pre-determined careers after graduating. 13 of these were Army officers who had between 3 and 6 years service before coming up; 18 were R.N. officers who had done 1 year as naval cadets before being sent to Cambridge as part of their naval training. Some of the remaining 18 men had done their National Service after graduation, and had remained in the Forces after they finished their National Service.

Journalism, art and entertainment. More than half the 48 men in this group were editors, journalists or authors. About a quarter were working in various capacities in radio, television, theatre or films, and about a quarter were musicians.

To complete the picture, we need to show how qualifications and occupations are linked. Table 19 shows how the graduates in the different subjects were distributed by their type of employment. In order that the position of the non-medical scientist can be seen more easily, the table excludes doctors.

Not unexpectedly, the engineering graduates were mainly in industry, with small groups in the Forces and in private practice as civil and other engineering consultants. The number of scientists in industry and education was similar, with rather few in any of the other employment groups except the Scientific Civil Service (29 including the Government Research Institutes and a further 13 in the U.K.A.E.A.). Scientific posts in universities and in many research establishments would often be open only to Ph.D.s. Certainly almost all the scientists employed in these places had doctorates or Part II of the natural sciences tripos. Among the teachers of science in schools, however, there were only two Ph.D.s: and not more than half had taken a part II.

Mathematicians were in various types of employment. 28 had obtained Ph.D.s and were in university posts; 19 had qualified as accountants or actuaries, and most of these were in industry and commerce. Several were doing work in connection with computer programming. The economists were mainly in industry and commerce; 12 of them had qualified as actuaries.

It is not only would-be solicitors and barristers who read Law, and for many graduates it is as much a background subject as one of the other arts. Just over half the law graduates qualified as solicitors or barristers; most of these were in private practice at the time of the survey; 19 were in government service, and 15 in industry. Almost all the other law graduates were in industry and commerce, mostly in general management, and 30 qualified as chartered accountants after graduating.

The other arts subjects were represented in all the employment groups, industry, commerce and the schools being the largest groups. Comparatively few arts graduates obtained a higher degree after graduating, and almost all the 28 who had a Ph.D. were in university posts.

The relationship between subject and occupation can be looked at in two ways. The question 'What happens to arts graduates?' can be answered by looking at the way in which each subject is distributed among the main employment groups. It is in those terms that we have commented on Table 19. Diagram (*a*) shows the percentages in diagrammatic

TABLE 19. *Degree Subject by Employment Group: Men working in the United Kingdom*[1]

Employment group	Degree subject							Total
	Engineering	Natural Science	Mathematics	Agriculture Estate Management and Architecture	Law	Economics and Social Anthropology	Other arts	
Industry	133	119	36	17	67	30	113	514
Commerce	3	4	12	15	44	16	86	180
Professional practices other than medicine	36	9	7	32	133	10	36	263
Church	2	8	3	—	6	1	101	121
Schools	8	51	22	3	11	3	236	334
Universities, training and technical colleges	11	67	29	1	5	5	70	188
Civil service	2	11	6	4	5	2	42	72
Local government	4	—	—	4	17	—	7	32
Industrial research establishments	10	16	6	—	—	1	2	35
Government research institutes	2	18	1	—	—	—	2	23
U.K.A.E.A.	7	13	6	—	1	—	2	29
Forces	31	11	—	—	3	—	5	50
Journalism, art and entertainment	3	3	1	2	6	1	32	48
Agriculture	2	7	—	39	3	1	6	58
Total	254	329	129	117	301	70	740	1940

1. This table excludes doctors who read the natural sciences tripos before qualifying, and all men in the 'miscellaneous' employment group.

23

THE EMPLOYMENT OF CAMBRIDGE GRADUATES

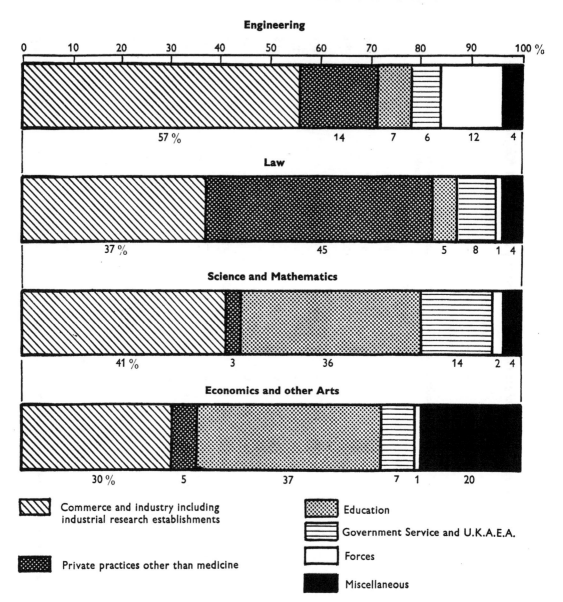

Diagram (a). Degree subject by employment group: men working in the United Kingdom (percentage of each subject).

form, bringing out the main differences between the subjects. Graduates who qualified in medicine are not included, nor those who read agriculture, estate management or architecture. Most of the graduates in agriculture were farming at the time of the survey; a few were teaching or employed in research and advisory posts in government service. The majority of those who read architecture or estate management were in private practice; a few were in industry and commerce, nine were in government service.

It is also interesting to look at each employment group separately, and see what proportions of the various subjects were employed in each. This is shown in diagram (b).

Industry had a higher proportion of graduates in engineering and science than in arts subjects. Commerce and private practices had a much higher proportion of arts men. 60% of those in education were arts graduates, with a higher proportion in schools than universities etc. (73% of the schoolteachers were arts graduates, 40% of the university and technical college teachers. Only 21% of the schoolteachers were scientists or mathematicians as against 51% of the university teachers). Taking local government, the civil service, and the U.K.A.E.A. together, there were almost equal proportions of arts graduates and of those in science plus technology, although there were very few engineers among the latter. The majority of the 14% who were law graduates were in the town clerk's departments of local authorities, and the 33% who read other arts subjects were administrative civil servants. The scientists and mathematicians were mainly in government research posts; about half of these had obtained a Ph.D. or a M.Sc. after graduating.

4. Type of work in industry

Within industry, there were some interesting differences in the occupations of men who had read different subjects.

The more specialised engineers and scientists (i.e. those who read part II of the natural sciences and mechanical sciences tripos) were more often in research and development jobs than those who had read part I only. Many of the research posts would not be open to part I graduates, and a higher proportion of these were in general management, production and sales departments. The higher management positions do not seem to be very often held by men who have been some time in research posts, the implication here being that in their early thirties fewer of the 'specialist' technicians and scientists seemed to be on the way to top management positions than the less specialised graduates, though we cannot say whether this remains true at a later stage in their careers.

It should be remembered that the general administration and management group covers a fairly wide range of jobs at different levels of responsibility. 37 out of the 84 men in general management had some qualification in addition to their Cambridge B.A. Six had qualified as chartered accountants, 9 as solicitors, 17 were members of professional bodies such as the Chartered Institute of Secretaries, the British Institute of Management or an engineering institution; the others included two with higher degrees. In general, those with additional qualifications appeared to be in higher management positions than those without, and most of them had reached these positions after a period in some other departments of industry; usually finance or production departments, some from sales, rather few from research departments.

There were almost as many law graduates in general management as all other arts put together; as already stated, 9 of them had additional legal qualifications. There were another

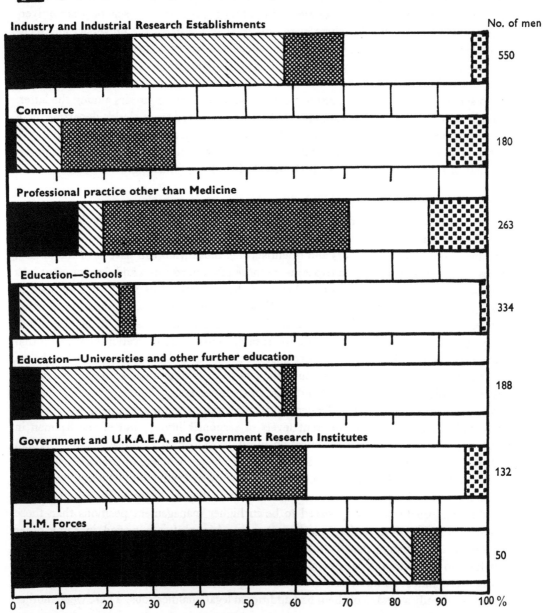

Diagram (*b*). Degree subject by employment group: men working in the United Kingdom (percentage of each group).

26

TABLE 20. *Men working in Industrial Concerns: Degree Subject by Type of Work*

Degree subject

Type of work	Engineering Studies and Mechanical Science I	Mechanical Science II and Chemical Engineering	Natural Science I	Natural Science II	Mathematics	Economics and Social Anthropology	Law	Other[1]	Total
General management	14	1	3	3	4	4	25	28	82
Production and operations	30	9	13	19	5	3	5	12	96
Accounting and finance	—	1	—	—	3	5	7	5	21
Sales, marketing and advertising	15	2	9	8	5	13	19	57	128
Research, design and development	32	22	9	44	16	4	2	8	137
Information, advisory and consultant	4	—	6	4	3	—	6	7	30
Personnel	—	1	—	1	—	1	2	11	16
Miscellaneous	2	—	—	—	—	—	1	2	5
Total in Industry	97	36	40	79	36	30	67	130	515
Industrial Research Establishments	2	8	2	14	6	1	—	2	35

1. Agriculture, estate management and architecture plus arts subjects other than economics, social anthropology and law.

6 qualified solicitors, shown under 'Information, advisory and consultant' work, who were specifically concerned with legal advice rather than general management. The information and advisory group also included two doctors and two land agents; the remainder were engaged in information and liaison work.

5. Occupation and class of degree

Not unexpectedly, the graduates who had obtained a First Class Honours degree were most often found in university research posts and university teaching.

TABLE 21. *Class of Degree by Employment Group: Men working in the United Kingdom*

(percentage of each degree class)

Employment group	Degree class						All classes percent	Number of men
	I	2.i	2.ii	2 undivided	3	Ordinary		
Industry	14	15	20	36	30	32	24	515
Commerce	3	9	9	7	10	10	8	180
Private practices and medicine	14	21	27	13	20	9	20	438
Research establishments	9	4	4	6	3	1	4	93
Schools	5	20	18	5	15	22	15	334
Universities, etc.	35	12	4	9	3	1	9	188
Civil service	11	5	3	3	1	} 1 {	3	74
Local government	3	2	1	2	1		2	33
Other	6	16	14	19	17	24	15	328
Total percentage	100	100	100	100	100	100	100	
Total number of men	206	388	620	240	589	140		2183

The universities (9% or all the graduates) had 35% of the First Class Honours. The Civil Service also had more than its share of firsts; with only 3% of all the graduates, it had 11% of the firsts. On the other hand, schoolteachers (15% of the graduates) included only 5% with First Class Honours. The 2.i classes were more evenly distributed, schools having a relatively high proportion; on the other hand the schools also had a relatively high proportion of graduates with Ordinary degrees, as did industry and commerce. Academic attainment is, of course, not the only standard by which the graduates' ability should be judged, or necessarily the most important. In some occupations, and school-teaching is probably one, temperament and personality are of at least equal, sometimes greater importance.

Table 22 shows the distribution of degree class for men in different types of work in industry and in research establishments.

In this table, the percentages are calculated across the table, to show the relative proportions of different classes in each department. Comparison of the Second Class Honours men is difficult because of the number who had an undivided second class in engineering; the highest proportion of these were in the research and development departments. It is interesting to note the high proportion of men with First Class Honours in general management; this is greater than in any of the other industrial departments, and only just below the proportion in the industrial research establishments. Somewhat surprisingly, general management also had the highest proportion of Third Class and Ordinary degrees, with a correspondingly lower proportion of seconds. Among the research establishments, the Atomic Energy Authority appeared to have exceptionally high academic standards; and the industrial research establishments had relatively more firsts and fewer thirds than any of the departments in industry, including research and design.

TABLE 22. *Class of Degree by Type of Work: Men working in the United Kingdom*

(percentage of each type)

Type of work	Degree class						Total	
	I	2.i	2.ii	2 undivided	3	Ordinary	Percentage	Number
General management	10	8	23	10	38	11	100	82
Production	3	10	20	22	39	6	100	96
Sales	2	14	34	9	30	11	100	128
Research and development	7	10	17	30	31	5	100	137
Other	5	17	32	8	30	8	100	72
All industry	5	11	24	17	34	9	100	515
Industrial research establishments	11	14	24	28	23	—	100	35
Government research institutes	17	24	34	3	21	—	100	29
U.K.A.E.A.	34	10	24	14	10	7	100	29

CHAPTER IV

THE REWARDS OF WORK:
EARNINGS AND SATISFACTION

In this chapter we review what the graduates earned in the various occupations discussed in the previous chapter. Salary is, of course, only one of the returns most people hope for from their work. The scope of the work itself, the contacts and opportunities it provides, and the social usefulness of the job are all things which are for many people as important, often more important, than the financial reward. However, for almost everyone, earning is a basic necessity, and for many the main incentive towards working, and for the survey worker it is the only objective measure of progress. We also review in this chapter the information the graduates gave about their satisfaction with their work. This is not capable of objective measure, but to some extent it indicates the feelings of the graduates about their work as a whole.

1. Current earnings

If we wish to make comparisons of the earnings of men in different employment groups, some account should be taken of the variable amounts of additional emoluments which accompany basic pay. Most of the data on current earnings is given in terms of a 'total' value which includes the value of any fringe benefits. We also refer later to 'basic earnings'. These terms are defined below.

(a) *Total earnings*. This consists of basic salary before tax, plus the value of any additional emoluments. Ideally the total value of earnings should be taken as the total cost to the employer, i.e. it should include all money paid by the employer into any superannuation fund and for any allowances and non-cash benefits. The actual cost to the employer of non-cash benefits is, however, very difficult to ascertain, and beyond the scope of a postal survey of this nature. The benefits vary widely in type and value, and the majority of employees have little idea of their real cost. Most of them, however, have some idea of the value to themselves, and in Question 4, Section C, we asked the graduates to give this value ('the net amount of salary you would expect to compensate you if the benefits were not available').

The majority of respondents gave what appeared to be a reasonably realistic figure in these terms, although probably rather lower than the actual cost to the employer (particularly in the case of housing and board and lodging). This value, plus the employer's contribution to superannuation, was added to basic salary, and enabled us to place the total within a range of values with reasonable confidence; it would clearly be misleading to try to arrive at any precise value. There were inevitably a few borderline cases where the final total might reasonably have been just above or just below the dividing line between two value groups. In these cases the lower value group was assigned. The value of total earnings is a minimum value, and may be an underestimate in some cases; it does, however, make some allowance for the varying amounts of fringe benefits available in different employment groups.

(b) *Basic earnings.* This is salary before deduction of income tax, excluding family or marriage allowances, benefits in kind and superannuation, but including any annual bonus payments in cash. The latter were included because they are regularly paid by some industrial and commercial concerns, and may make an appreciable addition to the basic salary. Family or marriage allowances were excluded from basic salary in order to eliminate differences due solely to marital status and number of children; they were included in the value of additional emoluments.

This distinction between basic and total earnings applies only to salaried employees. For the self-employed the same figure was used throughout—this was the total annual earnings from the business or practice, excluding non-taxable expenses incurred in the running of the business, but before the deduction of income tax. (Question 6, Section D.)

TABLE 23. *Distribution of Total Earnings by Employment Status: Graduates working full-time in the United Kingdom*

(percentage of each group)

	Total earnings: £ per year								Total percentage	Total graduates
	Under 1000	1000– 1249	1250– 1499	1500– 1749	1750– 1999	2000– 2499	2500– 2999	3000 and over		
Self-employed men	12	9	7	12	11	18	10	21	100	289
Men employed in family business	3	3	4	13	4	15	10	48	100	72
Other employed men	10	16	21	21	13	12	4	3	100	1793
1952/1953 women	24	42	19	7	4	4	—	—	100	75
1937/1938 women	18	16	22	15	10	9	5	5	100	79

Table 23 shows the distribution of total earnings of men working in the United Kingdom by employment status, and includes the women graduates working full-time for comparison. 73% of the men employed in a family business were earning over £2000 p.a., 48% over £3000. 49% of the self-employed were earning over £2000, 21% over £3000. Of the employed men, 17% were earning more than £2000, only 3% over £3000. The financial advantages of joining a family business or becoming self-employed seem to be obvious, but three things need to be remembered.

First, these figures are weighted in favour of the family business and self-employed because the majority of them were working in industry, commerce and private professional practices. A quarter of the employed men were working in schools or one of the Churches— the two lowest paid occupation groups. None the less, there were marked differences within the same employment groups, as Table 24 shows.

Secondly, many more of the self-employed and men in a family business have got nearer the top of the hierarchies of their particular concerns than the employed men—several of them are already at the top. This means that any future increase in earnings depends more on the expansion of their business (or their share in the business). The employed men can hope for future promotions or the sale of their services to a higher bidder, or the possibility of entering partnerships themselves. Many of them may catch up eventually, and it does not follow that the disparity in earnings will be as great in some years time as it is now.

Thirdly, although there is a smaller proportion of self-employed and family business men in the lower earnings groups, there are still quite a number—a slightly higher proportion of the self-employed were earning under £1000 than in the other two groups, and

TABLE 24. *Total Earnings of Men employed in Industry and Commerce: Men employed in a Family Business v. Other Employed*

(percentage of each group)

	Total earnings: £ per year				Total percentage	Number of men
	Under 1500	1500–1999	2000–2999	3000 and over		
Industry:						
Employed in family business	7	18	20	55	100	46
Other employed	24	43	28	5	100	453
Commerce:						
Employed in family business	17	22	17	44	100	18
Other employed	23	47	24	6	100	127

there were several earning nothing, or less than £500. There is, in fact, a much greater range of earnings in these two groups than among the employed men. The risks involved in free-lance work or partnerships are greater and although there may be a better chance of earning more at an earlier age, there is also a greater chance of earning very little.

Comparing the men with the women, Table 23 shows that 71% of the employed men were earning between £1000 and £2000, and so were 72% of the women graduating at the same time, but with a much higher proportion of the women earning less than £1250, and only 4% (3 women) earning over £2000 as against 18% of the employed men. The spread of earnings was more uniform for the 1937–1938 women compared with the younger women and more like that of the men, but it has to be remembered that the 1937/1938 women graduated 15 years earlier, and are mostly now in their forties. To some extent the relatively lower earnings of the women are a reflection of the fact that very few of them were employed in industry, commerce or professional practices, other than medicine, whereas the majority of the highest-earning men were in these fields (three quarters of those earning £2500 or more.) All but one of the older women graduates earning more than £2000 were in education (universities or schools), the Civil Service or medicine.

Table 25 and diagram (c) show the distribution of total earnings by type of employment for the men.

The effect of standardised salary scales is clearly seen in the relatively narrow range of earnings of the majority of men in public service fields (education, government service, medicine and the forces). Schoolteachers stand out as being the lowest paid group apart from the Church, with 75% earning between £1000 and £1500. 36% of university and technical college teachers had reached the £1500–£2000 range, but only 7% were earning

TABLE 25. *Distribution of Total Earnings by Employment Group: Men working in the United Kingdom*[1]

(percentage of each type of employment)

	Earnings group: £ per year									
	Under 1000	1000– 1249	1250– 1499	1500– 1749	1750– 1999	2000– 2499	2500– 2999	3000 and over	Total per- centage	Number in group
Industry	2	7	14	24	16	18	9	9	100	510
Distributive trades	3	5	10	23	17	21	5	16	100	71
Insurance, banking and finance	3	4	17	17	21	19	4	15	100	104
Schools	14	40	35	7	1	2	—	1	100	327
Universities, technical, training colleges	8	12	37	25	11	6	1	—	100	187
Local government	9	12	18	24	24	12	—	—	100	33
Civil service	—	8	19	22	16	32	3	—	100	73
Churches	79	19	2	—	—	—	—	—	100	114
Medicine	1	13	18	38	12	12	3	3	100	173
Law	8	17	9	12	8	18	9	18	100	127
Other professional practices	5	10	15	15	14	16	12	13	100	137
Journalism, art and entertainment	19	11	8	11	15	17	13	6	100	47
Agriculture	35	9	7	5	5	14	9	16	100	57
Research establishments	1	7	12	39	19	16	4	2	100	93
Forces	—	6	16	24	30	24	—	—	100	50
Miscellaneous	10	10	21	25	14	8	6	6	100	46
All United Kingdom men	10	14	19	20	12	13	5	7	100	2149

[1] This table excludes 5 National Servicemen, 21 men who were working part-time or who were temporarily unemployed, and 21 men for whom total earnings are not known.

more than this. There were 32 graduates in the administrative civil service, 25 of them earning over £2000 (the 32% in the £2000–£2500 range shown in Table 25); whereas none of the scientific and technical civil servants were earning over £2000. These include 29 men in government research establishments and 9 in various departments of the Scientific Civil Service. 18 of these 38 men had a Ph.D., 4 had an M.Sc. and 3 had a year's further study after graduation, so that most of them would have started their career employment later than the graduates in the administrative branches. The results from this rather small group of graduates suggest that promotion in the Scientific Civil Service is slower than in the administrative Civil Service.

3

THE EMPLOYMENT OF CAMBRIDGE GRADUATES

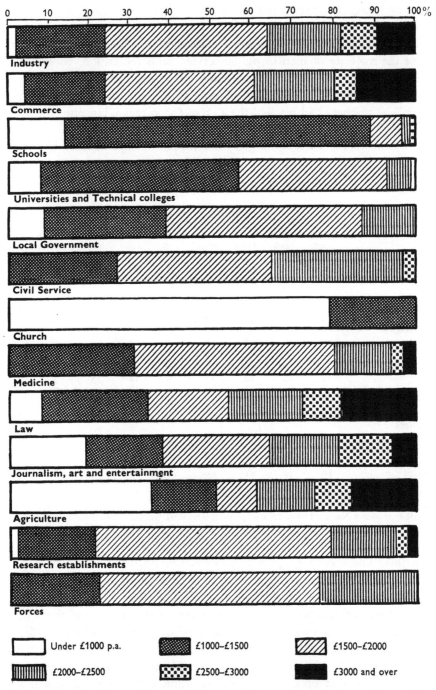

Diagram (*c*). Distribution of total earnings by employment group: men working in the United Kingdom.

34

There is much greater variation of earnings among the private fields of employment. Agriculture is particularly outstanding, with marked concentrations at both the top and bottom of the income scale (the majority being self-employed at both ends). But although the men in industry, commerce, law, journalism, entertainment and private practices generally were more heavily concentrated in the middle income groups, each of these occupations had more than a third with earnings over £2000.

Total earnings have been shown only in distribution tables because, as we said earlier,

TABLE 26. *Basic Earnings: Graduates working in the United Kingdom*

	Annual earnings: £				Number of men
	Average	Median	Lower quartile	Upper quartile	
Men—by employment group:					
Industry	1840	1590	1370	2100	511
Distributive trades	1950	1670	1400	2000	70
Insurance, banking and finance	2110	1650	1320	2110	104
Schools	1100	1100	990	1225	329
Universities	1310	1260	1150	1460	151
Technical colleges	1320	1370	1095	1500	27
Local government	1450	1430	1305	1700	33
Civil service	1560	1590	1260	1870	73
Churches	630	625	590	750	120
Medicine	1520	1400	1250	1665	172
Law—barristers	2100	1560	1075	2750	35
Law—solicitors	1960	1775	1200	2500	90
Journalism, art and entertainment	1580	1540	1070	2000	48
Agriculture	1682	1500	800	2250	56
Research establishments	1635	1550	1390	1785	93
Forces	1180	1190	950	1405	50
Men—by employment status:					
Self-employed	2145	2000	1315	2500	288
Employed in family business	2800	2500	1760	3800	71
Other employed	1424	1350	1100	1650	1789
All men	1566	1425	1150	1790	2147
All women working full-time					
1952/1953	1125	1080	950	1250	74
1937/1938	1570	1455	1080	1900	79

a very precise evaluation of additional emoluments was not possible. The differences between employment groups are perhaps brought out more clearly if average, median, and quartile values are compared. These have been calculated from basic earnings (i.e. excluding additional emoluments), since these were reasonably precise figures. Table 26 and the accompanying diagram (*d*) show the results of these calculations. No calculations have been made for groups of under 20 graduates, and it must be emphasised that the figures for the small occupation groups which are shown are not necessarily typical of that occupation as a whole.

Table 27 shows the basic salary values for salaried employees in different types of work within industry. The family business men and the self-employed are excluded in order to

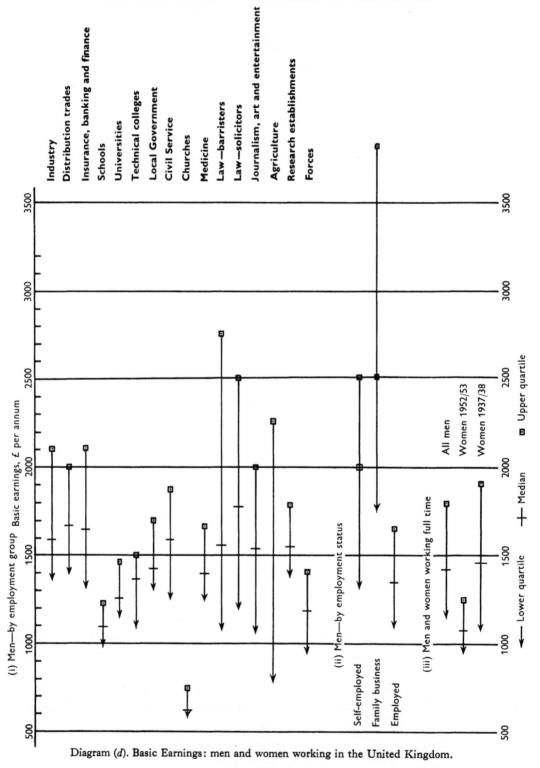

Diagram (*d*). Basic Earnings: men and women working in the United Kingdom.

show the position of the graduates who did not have special opportunities for earning high amounts.

The graduates in research and development departments (i.e. those not working in independent research establishments) were not only earning less on average than the other men, but also had a narrower dispersion of earnings. The inter-quartile range for

TABLE 27. *Basic Earnings by Type of Work in Industry: Men working in the United Kingdom*

(Salaried employees only, excluding those in a family business)

Type of work	Basic salary: £ per year				Number of men
	Average	Median	Lower quartile	Upper quartile	
General management	2000	1600	1250	2200	46[1]
Production and operation	1770	1605	1440	1930	94
Sales and marketing	1860	1740	1350	2250	109
Research, design and development departments	1650	1550	1350	1750	134
Industrial research establishments	1640	1590	1395	1900	34

[1] The 82 graduates in general management in industry included 11 who were self-employed and 25 who were employed in a family business.

these men was £400, as against £490 for those in production, £900 for those in sales, and £950 for those in general management. Those in industrial research establishments also had lower average and median earnings, but had a greater spread of earnings, the upper quartile approaching that of the production departments.

2. Earnings and class of degree

Academic success did not necessarily bring the highest financial rewards.

Men with a First Class Honours degree, or a 2.i were less likely to be in the lower earnings group than those with lower class degrees. 10% of the firsts and 25% of the 2.i.s were earning less than £1250, as against 30% of the Third Class Honours men and 34% of those with Ordinary degrees. On the other hand, a smaller proportion of the firsts and 2.i.s were

TABLE 28. *Total Earnings by Class of Degree: Men working in the United Kingdom*

Total earnings: £ per year	(percentage of each degree class) Degree class						All United Kingdom men	Number of men
	I	2.i	2.ii	2 undivided	3	Ordinary		
Under 1250	10	25	27	14	30	34	25	544
1250–1499	19	22	20	16	18	14	19	405
1500–1999	39	33	30	43	27	24	32	680
2000–2499	23	11	10	13	14	16	13	284
2500 and over	9	9	13	14	11	12	11	245
Total percentage	100	100	100	100	100	100	100	
Total number	204	384	616	240	577	137		2158

earning £2500 or over—9% as against 11% or 12% of the Third Class and Ordinary degrees. There is not a great deal of difference in the distribution of the middle range of earnings between £1250 and £2500, except that the First Class Honours men were more often in the £2000–£2500 group than the rest. There is, in fact, no direct relationship between degree class and earnings, and the figures in Table 28 are a reflection of the earnings in particular occupation groups. We have already seen that 35% of the men with First Class Honours were in university posts, and 20% of those with 2.i.s were in school-teaching; 36% of university teachers were earning between £1500 and £1999, and 89% of school-teachers were earning less than £1500. There is an obvious connection between these figures and the distribution of earnings in Table 28. We cannot therefore discuss earnings in terms of degree class as such. Men with certain classes tend to go into certain occupations, and it is the occupation which determines earnings rather than the class of degree. With a larger sample, it would be interesting to see how salary varied between men with different classes in the same occupations, but in this sample, when the occupation groups are broken down into degree classes and earnings, the numbers become too small for any significant differences to emerge.

3. Earnings and degree subject

The same difficulty applies when considering the earnings of graduates who read particular subjects; the overall picture is obscured by weightings due to occupation groups with a narrow range of earnings. An analysis of earnings by degree subject for four of the largest occupation groups in industry (the largest employment group without standardised salary scales) revealed no marked differences between the subjects, and the numbers were too small for any significance to be attached to the results. The only conclusion that was possible was that the small number of arts graduates who were in research and planning occupations did rather less well than the scientists and engineers—a not unexpected result.

4. Earnings and post-graduate qualifications

Appendix III shows the total earnings of men with various post-graduate qualifications. This reflects the tendencies we have already seen. Those who were working in industry, commerce and private practices had a greater spread of earnings, with higher upper quartile values. The earnings of Ph.D.s were conditioned mainly by the fact that the majority were in occupations with fixed rates of pay—research posts and university teaching. It must also be borne in mind that they had had less time in employment than those with no post-graduate qualifications.

5. Additional emoluments

So far we have discussed basic earnings and total earnings including other emoluments. It is interesting, also, to look at the type and value of these additional benefits and the sorts of employment in which they occur.

5% of the salaried employees not in a family business had no additional emoluments at all, the highest proportion in professional practices other than medicine. 87% belonged to a superannuation scheme and 49% had additional emoluments other than superannuation. The proportions were reversed among those in a family business; only 44% of these belonged to a superannuation scheme, but 72% had other fringe benefits. The relative proportions are given below. 'Other' emoluments cover all benefits other than superannuation, i.e. family and marriage allowances and non-cash benefits.

TABLE 29. *Type of Additional Emoluments*

(percentage of each group)[1]

	Men employed in non-family concerns	Men employed in family businesses
No emoluments	5	11
Contributory pension scheme only	37 } 69	7 } 21
Contributory pension scheme and other emoluments	32	14
Non-contributory pension scheme only	7 } 19	1 } 23
Non-contributory pension scheme and other emoluments	12	22
Other emoluments only	5	36
Not known	2	9
Total percentage	100	100
Total number of men	1789	73

[1] Excluding 21 men who were temporarily unemployed or in part-time work.

Several of the men who did not belong to superannuation schemes were in non-established or temporary posts in government service and universities, or had only recently taken up jobs in industry or commerce, and expected to become eligible for superannuation in the future. In the professional practices provision for superannuation was less common.

Table 30 shows how the value of additional emoluments varied between different employment groups—the values expressed as a percentage of total earnings.

This table excludes men employed in agriculture, journalism, arts, entertainment, National Service, the 'miscellaneous' group, and the men who were unemployed or in part-time work.

There were 345 men for whom no evaluation is shown in Table 30. In most of these cases there was sufficient information about the kind of benefits to enable us to place total earnings within a range of values (see the first page of this chapter), but not enough to allow us to assign a more precise value to the emoluments. The majority of unknown values were in industry and commerce, where a number of men had no idea of their employer's contribution to the superannuation scheme. Most people are interested in what they have to contribute themselves, rather fewer in what kind of pension they will get eventually, but very many take the employer's contribution for granted and do not know the details unless it is one of the standard contributory schemes (universities, schools, local government and the National Health Service).

The Churches and the Forces received the highest proportion of their earnings as additional emoluments. In the Churches the greater part of this was free housing, which with a low rate of basic pay gives a high percentage of additional emoluments, though not a high level of total earnings. The Forces have a much higher amount of cash allowances than the other groups (marriage and education allowances for example), and all have subsidised housing and board. In the other employment groups, the majority of men had

TABLE 30. *Value of Additional Emoluments by Employment Group: Salaried Employees (Men working in the United Kingdom.)*

Employer's contribution to superannuation plus other additional emoluments

(percentage of each type of employment)

		Additional emoluments: percentage of total earnings					Number in group	Per-centage
	Nil	1–6 per cent	7–12 per cent	13–19 per cent	20–29 per cent	30 per cent and over		
Industry	7	39	32	14	7	1	334	100
Commerce	8	23	28	20	20	1	76	100
Schools	—	64	11	12	9	4	308	100
Universities	2	—	53	37	8	—	154	100
Training and technical colleges	3	85	6	3	—	3	33	100
Local government	—	67	6	18	9	—	33	100
Civil service	3	—	—	91	6	—	71	100
U.K.A.E.A. and government research institutes	2	—	82	15	2	—	56	100
Churches	—	4	11	20	40	25	108	100
Medicine	1	1	77	12	8	1	104	100
Professional practices	40	30	17	5	6	2	101	100
Forces	—	—	2	6	18	74	50	100
Total percentage	5	30	29	19	11	6		100
Total number in group	80	428	408	275	154	84	1428	

no very substantial benefits other than superannuation; the latter accounts for the greater part of the values shown in Table 25. The employer's share in contributory schemes was most often between 5% and 10% of basic salary, and of the order of 15% in non-contributory schemes. Industry and commerce provided the greatest variety of other fringe benefits. The most common were subsidised meals, car allowances, travel allowances and help with housing and removal expenses. A number of doctors in hospital posts received board and lodging, but only a few men in the other groups. Only a few men (apart from those in the Forces and the Churches) were living in rent-free or subsidised houses. Again excluding the Forces and the ministers of religion, 67% of the men receiving fringe benefits valued them at under £175, 6% at £375 or over. The young industrial or commercial executive living on an expense account and driving the firm's Bentley does not seem to be well represented in this group of Cambridge graduates. Some men were receiving generous benefits but only a small minority.

6. Satisfactions

In the first part of this chapter we have discussed the money returns the graduates received for their work. We consider now the less tangible rewards. Not everyone is fortunate enough to have a job which is both well-paid and satisfying in other respects, and many people have to put up with deficiencies in one respect in order to achieve other things which seem important.

There are bound to be divergent views about what constitutes 'good' pay, and what other aspects of a job are important. However, the extent to which a man feels satisfied by his own standards may be an important influence in determining how he does his work and whether or not he stays in the same job. With a shortage of qualified men and women in several fields of employment, these considerations have a more than purely personal importance. We cannot attempt any profound analysis of the causes and effects of satisfaction, but we can give a very general idea of which graduates were happy in their work, and which were obviously dissatisfied. The questions on satisfactions were designed to find out first, what the graduate felt about his salary, and secondly, what he felt about his work in general.

Satisfaction with salary cannot, of course, be singled out from other satisfactions as being necessarily more important, nor as an entirely separate cause of satisfaction, but we have treated it separately because it can be related to something which can be measured—the actual rate of pay—whereas other satisfactions cannot be related to a specific standard.

7. What is a fair return?

Opinions vary widely as to how far salaries are equitable in particular occupation groups, although current discussions about the earnings of the teaching profession suggest that there is considerable support for the view that in this field at least there is room for improvement. Question 6, Section C, asked the employed graduates, 'Do you feel that your present salary gives you a fair return for the work you do?' Those who answered 'No' were asked to say what they felt would be a reasonable salary for their present job. Answers to this question are bound to be subjective, and allow scope for wishful thinking, but can be used to see if there are any obvious trends of opinion among particular groups of the graduates. The question was not put to self-employed men because it cannot be answered in the same terms in their case. Their earnings depend to a far greater extent on their individual exertions and capabilities, much less on current rates of pay within particular occupation groups.

Table 31 shows how men in various employment groups answered this question.

Those recorded as 'unable to say' include those who did not answer the question at all—a much higher proportion in the medical profession than in other fields—and those who specifically objected to the question, on two rather opposing grounds. One group held that they (and, they suggested, most people) would probably always feel they ought to have higher earnings and had no idea whether their salaries were fair or not; the other group felt the question inappropriate, suggesting that pay was an unimportant consideration to them, and that they could not relate it to standards of 'fairness'. The latter group understandably included a relatively high proportion of men employed in the Church, and we recognise that the question must seem inappropriate to people whose work is so specifically vocational. Not unexpectedly, the highest proportion of those dissatisfied with their present salary were schoolteachers, although a nearly equal number were satisfied. Teaching is, of course, vocational to a considerable extent, and even among those who thought their salaries were too low there were many who found the vocational aspect a sufficient compensation. The median salary of the schoolteachers was £1100; the increases they said

TABLE 31. *Satisfaction with Salary—Men working in the United Kingdom: Salaried employees only (excluding men employed in a family business)*[1]

(percentage of each employment group)

Employment group	'Does your salary give a fair return?'			Total	
	Yes	No	Unable to say	Percentage	Number of men
Schools	43	48	9	100	328
Local government	58	36	6	100	33
Universities, training and technical colleges	57	35	8	100	188
Medicine	47	31	22	100	119
Professional practices other than medicine	68	31	1	100	136
Industry	73	25	2	100	458
Churches	40	21	39	100	121
Civil service	72	21	7	100	74
Commerce	78	19	3	100	132
Regular Forces	82	18	—	100	50
Research institutes	86	14	—	100	93
Journalism, art and entertainment	87	13	—	100	29
All salaried employees	65	30	5	100	1761

[1] This table excludes men employed in agriculture, National Service, and miscellaneous occupations, and the unemployed men (59 men altogether).

would be reasonable were fairly evenly spread throughout the range £100–£499, with 7% suggesting between £500–£799, and 3% over £800. Only 2 men thought an addition of £1000 or more would be fair.*

Rather fewer—35%—of university and technical college teachers were dissatisfied with their salaries. (Current median £1260.) The highest proportion of suggested increases fell between £200 and £399—4% suggested more than £800. In both medicine and the other private professional practices almost all who suggested increases of over £500 specified amounts of under £800. There were no very marked differences between the answers from the men in the other employment groups.

An obvious question that arises is how far satisfaction with earnings is related to the existing salary level; we might expect the lower paid employees to be more often dis-

* All increases have been related to basic salary, i.e. salary excluding any additional emoluments.

satisfied and to think in terms of relatively larger increases, irrespective of where they were working. This was certainly the general trend among these graduates, the proportion of those who did not think their salary gave them a fair return decreasing inversely with basic earnings. Everyone earning over £3000 said they were getting a fair return, 50% of those with under £1000 said they were not, 43% of men earning between £1000 and £1500 were dissatisfied, and 12% of those with £2000–£3000.

There was a tendency for those with higher basic earnings to suggest relatively lower increases, when these are calculated as a percentage increase on current salary. Half those earning under £1000 thought they deserved an increase of 50% or more, only a third thought it should be less than 40%. The majority of those earning £1500 or more thought they would be content with an increase of between 10% and 30%. Those earning between £1000 and £1500 mostly suggested increases between 10% and 40%.

We have little evidence to indicate how far the graduates' conception of a reasonable salary was based on current levels within their particular field of work, or the extent to which they were influenced by their knowledge of salaries in other fields. A few men qualified their answers by saying that they thought their salaries were fair in relation to others in their own profession, but that the profession as a whole was underpaid. In general about two-thirds of all the men thought that their salaries were fair; although several made the point that they could always do with a little more. It would have been interesting to know if any men felt themselves to be overpaid, but the chances of obtaining an objective answer to this seemed rather remote; two men, however, very honestly volunteered the information.

8. Satisfaction in general

At Question 8, Section C, we listed ten possible sources of satisfaction or dissatisfaction, including, again, salary, and asked the graduate to indicate how far his current job satisfied him by allocating a score to each factor he considered important; he was also invited to add any other factors, not listed, which he considered important. The scores ranged from +3, very satisfied, to −3, very dissatisfied. From this we hoped to gain a general picture of the kind of satisfaction the graduates looked for, and the extent to which their jobs supplied these. Interpretation of the results can only be made in very general terms since there are inevitable variations in interpretation of both question and answers, but the results do indicate at least which graduates had fairly strong feelings about their working conditions. The number of items to which a score was allocated varied between 5 and 13, and the overall satisfaction score is the total score recorded by the graduate as a percentage of the maximum possible score for those items he considered important. This means that we are giving equal weight to each source specified, whereas the respondent may not in fact do so. For this reason, we have shown only the extreme ends of the scale—the obviously satisfied as distinct from the obviously dissatisfied. We do not feel that any useful purpose would be served by trying to discern shades of intermediate satisfaction. It is worth noting that when the questionnaires were being coded, it was usually possible to forecast from the general tone of the comments at various points whether the graduate was likely to have a very high or a very low satisfaction score.

Table 32 shows how these scores varied between the men who were known to be employed in a family business, the other salaried employees, and the self-employed.

Table 32. *Satisfaction score by Employment Status: Men working in the United Kingdom*

(percentage of each group of graduates)[1]

Employment status	Dissatisfied			Satisfied	Not known	Total	
	Negative scores	0–24	25–74	75–100		Percentage	Number
Self-employed	1	8	52	34	5	100	290
Employed in family business	3	10	46	36	5	100	73
Other employed	4	11	55	23	7	100	1810

[1] The scale used in scoring each item was as follows:

+3 very satisfied   −3 very dissatisfied
+2 moderately satisfied   −2 rather dissatisfied
+1 just satisfied   −1 slightly dissatisfied
0 No particular feelings

This suggests that the self-employed men were less likely to be dissatisfied than the others, and more likely to be very satisfied than the employed men. Those in a family business were more often satisfied. The rather large intermediate range includes some who were moderately satisfied and some who were slightly dissatisfied. The self-employed and family business men tended to have higher scores in this range than the salaried employees.

Table 33 compares the scores for the salaried employees in some of the main employment groups—here, again, we are only picking out the extremes. It is interesting to see that the schools and government service had the lowest proportion of dissatisfied men, and that the schools had at least their fair share of men who were satisfied. Industry had more dissatisfied and fewer satisfied men than any other group, but the differences particularly among the dissatisfied were not of a substantial order.

TABLE 33. *Comparative Satisfaction Score in Employment Groups: Salaried employees only (excluding those in a family business) (Men working in the United Kingdom)*

(percentage of each employment group)

Employment group	Dissatisfied			Satisfied
	Negative score	0–24	25–74	75–100
Industry	7	13	64	16
Commerce	3	15	55	27
Professional practices and medicine	3	16	60	21
Research establishments	7	7	59	27
Schools	3	8	64	25
Universities, etc.	2	12	56	30
Government service[1]	4	7	67	22
Forces[2]	4	11	65	22

[1] Civil service and local government.
[2] Excluding those (5) in National Service, who all had a negative score.

44

CHAPTER V

THE PAST AND THE FUTURE

The previous two chapters described the position of the men working in the United Kingdom at the time of the survey. In this chapter we consider the various routes by which they came to these positions, and give what evidence we have about their future expectations.

1. After graduation

Just over half the men found employment within 6 months of graduating in 1952 or 1953. 794 men went on to full-time study, and 134 went into the Armed Forces to do National Service.

TABLE 34. *Position within 6 Months of Graduation*

(percentage of men)

Permanent employment	53
Full-time study	36
National Service	4 ⎫ 6
National Service followed by full-time study	2 ⎭
Temporary work	2
Other	2
Not known	1
	——
	100

A small number (72) spent more than 6 months finding a post, and 33 of these took temporary jobs* while waiting for a permanent appointment. 17 were either having a prolonged vacation travelling abroad, or were still looking for a post. 22 had either been ill, or were otherwise prevented from starting work. All but 10 of these 72 men had found permanent employment within 18 months of graduation.

The number of men who did not go straight into paid employment or who did National Service after graduation was therefore little less than half the entire group. The length of time that elapsed before they could start their careers varied between 1 year and 5 years.

Those with a gap of up to $1\frac{1}{2}$ years are men who took Diplomas of Education, did theological training for one of the Ministries, or took other 1-year post-graduate diploma courses. Those with a gap of between 18 months and $2\frac{1}{2}$ years are mainly those who did National Service or 2-year post-graduate courses, apart from a few who followed National

---

* The distinction between a temporary and a permanent post was made on the basis of the type of job rather than the time the graduate remained in the job. Several men changed their employer after less than a year in their first job because of dissatisfaction, or a better opening offered elsewhere, but had not taken up the first job with the prior intention of changing it. These have been treated as going directly into a permanent job. The temporary posts were those which clearly bore no relationship to the graduate's future career, and were of a filling-in nature, such jobs as, for example, washers-up, or bus drivers. In these cases the graduates stated that they were waiting to take up a post for which they had already been accepted, or were still actively engaged in looking for a suitable permanent job.

Service with full-time study. Men studying for Ph.D.s and for medicine account for most of those with a gap of over $2\frac{1}{2}$ years. Not all the men who did a further full-time study course took up their first appointment immediately after the completion of their course. Some of them spent several months waiting for a post, having a holiday, etc., so that the total time between graduation and the first job was sometimes more than the length of the study course.

TABLE 35. *Total Time between Graduating and starting first Appointment*[1]

(percentage of men)

Under 6 months	53
6 months–$1\frac{1}{2}$ years	17
$1\frac{1}{2}$–$2\frac{1}{2}$ years	10
$2\frac{1}{2}$–$3\frac{1}{2}$ years	14
$3\frac{1}{2}$–$4\frac{1}{2}$ years	4
Over $4\frac{1}{2}$ years	1
Not known	1
	——
	100

[1] First appointment is used here to describe any paid employment other than National Service or purely casual jobs; it also includes articled clerkships and pupillages, whether paid or not.

TABLE 36. *Type of first Appointment*

(i) *Men who started paid employment within 6 months of graduation*[1]

	Number	Per cent
Articled clerkships	156	13
Graduate apprenticeships	143	12
Other	858	74
Not known	10	1
	——	——
	1167	100

(ii) *Men with some gap after graduation*

	Number	Per cent
Articled clerkships and pupillages	53	5
Graduate apprenticeships	14	1
Medical house jobs	188	19
Other	737	75
	——	——
	992	100

[1] Date of first appointment not known for 37 men.

There was therefore considerable variation in the time at which the graduates started their first appointment after graduation. This must be borne in mind when considering the kind of employment they first had; so must the fact that some of them were starting with various qualifications in addition to their first degree. A further variable is the conditions under which they were engaged in their first job. Some went into formal training appointments as articled clerks or apprentices, others into various jobs in industry as trainees, either in particular departments, or moving round several departments before being assigned to a particular niche. Others had no formal training on the job, but as one graduate put it, 'all experience is training and in that sense I am still a trainee'. Apart from those in apprenticeships or articles, we have not found it easy to differentiate between training and ordinary employment, particularly in industry. We did not ask for specific details of on-the-job training appointments, so it is hardly surprising that many of the answers did not make it clear whether or not the first appointment was specifically a training post. We have therefore distinguished only four types of first appointment. First, the articles or pupillages essential for qualification in accountancy and law, secondly, engineering apprenticeships, thirdly, pre-registration house jobs in medicine, and fourthly, all other posts.

2. Type of employment

Table 37 shows the employment group first entered by the graduate men, and compares the current employment position.

TABLE 37. *First Employment after graduating, and current Employment: Men working in the United Kingdom*

(percentage of each group)

| Employment group | First appointment after graduation | | | | | | Current appointment | |
| | No gap | | After some gap | | All first jobs | | | |
	Number	Per cent	Number	Per cent	Number	Per cent	Number	Per cent
Industry	453	39	120	12	573	26	515	24
Commerce	147	13	40	4	187	9	180	8
Professional practices:								
Accountancy	45	4	6	1	51	2	25	1
Law	88	8	33	3	121	6	126	6
Medicine	6	—	152	15	158	7	175	8
Other	66	6	20	2	86	4	112	5
All professional practices	205	18	211	21	416	19	438	20
Church	16	1	109	11	125	6	121	6
Research establishments	28	2	39	4	67	3	93	4
Schools	92	8	228	23	320	15	334	15
Universities and technical colleges	30	2	118	12	148	7	188	9
Civil service	56	5	32	3	88	4	74	3
Local government	20	2	15	1	35	2	33	2
Forces[1]	44	4	16	2	60	3	50	2
Other	74	6	64	7	138	6	157	7
Total percentage		100		100		100		100
Total number	1167		992		2157		2183[2]	
Not known					39			

[1] Excluding National Service.
[2] Excluding 13 who were temporarily unemployed.

47

The differences between the distribution of the graduates who went into their first job immediately after graduation and those who had some time-gap largely results from differences in various types of post-graduate training. The majority of those who went into industry did so immediately, including the engineers who started as graduate apprentices. The men who entered industry after some gap were mostly scientists who had done some further study (67 men) or men who had done National Service after graduation (38 men).

The graduates going into professional accountancy or law as articled clerks almost all did so immediately after graduation. Nearly all the 33 men who went into legal practices after some time-gap were barristers who had spent a year in full-time study before starting their pupillages. Most of the graduates taking first appointments in the universities, schools, and various religious Ministries did so after a period of further study. Most of those who were employed in government administrative posts, and the Income Tax Inspectorate, entered directly after graduation, whereas those entering Government service after a period of study were mainly scientists. 32 of the men in the Armed Forces had been sent to Cambridge as part of their military or naval training, and returned to their respective Services immediately after graduation. 10 of those who went in after some gap were men who started in National Service and after this signed on for a 3-year Short Service Commission; the remaining 6 were doctors who went straight into the Forces after qualifying.

There is very little difference in the overall distribution by employment group between first and current appointments. There are now slightly fewer graduates in industry and commerce, rather more in private practice, schools and universities, but in no case is there a difference of more than 2%. This is not to say that almost all the graduates have stayed in the same jobs, but rather that the changes between the various employment groups have resulted in a similar distribution in the end. Changes in employment since the first job are discussed later.

In Chapter III we related the graduate's current employment to his academic background, showing how the different degree classes and subjects were distributed among the main employment groups. There were no very great differences between the employment groups in respect of those factors at the time of first appointment.

3. Starting Salary

We have seen that 47% of the graduates did not go directly into a job after graduation, and that the time which elapsed before they started their careers varied from under a year up to 4 years or more. It therefore becomes difficult to make direct comparisons of starting salaries, since they relate to a series of different points in time. We would, for example, be comparing the men who first graduated in 1952 with those who had completed a 1-year post-graduate course in 1953, those who had finished National Service in 1954, and with the Ph.D.s in 1955, and so on. It does not seem reasonable to discount the effects of inflation and changing salary levels and make comparisons on the basis of occupation and qualification alone. But there are so many interrelated factors which determine salary levels, that to introduce further variables into a group as small as this would almost certainly obscure the issue and make interpretation extremely hazardous. The time factor cannot be ignored in any case, since at any given date the number of years the graduates have been in employment depends on when they started. It seemed better, however, to eliminate the variable date factor as far as possible, and taking the starting point to be graduation, to relate subsequent changes to this date. Salary levels are therefore compared at three points in time; first, the starting salaries of those who went into employment within 6 months of graduation; secondly, salaries 4 years after graduation; thirdly, current salary. Four years after graduation was chosen as a point at which the men who did further study or went into formal training schemes would almost all have completed their additional training. For many graduates of course this 4-year salary is, in fact, their starting salary, or only slightly above.

Starting salary therefore relates to the years 1952 and 1953; 4-year salary to 1956 and 1957, and current salary to 1961, the one year difference in graduation date being ignored throughout.

The data on starting salaries is not presented in order to make comparisons with those currently paid in various fields. There would be little value in this, since the starting point for many of these graduates is 7 or 8 years ago, and levels of pay have been increased in almost all fields of employment since that time. It is possible, however, to look at the relative levels within different occupation groups to see if there are any significant trends.

A number of graduates could not give figures for starting salary, and others gave figures for some, but not all of the subsequent years. This is not surprising in view of the time-span involved. Many have been able to give the information called for, but, because of the time-lag, the answers cannot be regarded as very precise. However, most of the figures were consistent with levels of pay at the time, and are probably reliable enough to show general trends.

Table 38 shows the starting salaries of the men who entered employment within 6 months of graduation. Apart from those who started as articled clerks, the majority were in the range £300–£599, rather more above than below £400.

The pay for graduate apprentices was not very different from that of other men going into industry, except that there was a higher proportion of apprentices in the £300–£399 range, rather fewer over £600. It is interesting to see that the salaries of schoolteachers compared very favourably with those of the other employment groups at that time (these were men who had not taken a post-graduate Diploma of Education), and that they had the highest proportion of men earning £600 and over. Unfortunately, many of these did not state what type of school their first appointment was in.

4. Four years

Four years after graduation most of the men had completed post-graduate training, and those who had gone into National Service had been in a job for about 2 years. We were interested to know whether the men who chose to delay the start of their careers by doing a period of full-time study after graduation lost financially by doing so. After they

4

TABLE 38. *Starting Salary by Type of first Appointment: Men working in the United Kingdom Men who took their 1st job within 6 months of graduation*[1]

(percentage of each employment group)

	\multicolumn{9}{c}{Starting salary: £ per year}	Total	
	Under 300	300–399	400–499	500–599	600–699	700–799	800–899	900–999	1000 and over	Percentage	Number
Graduate apprentices (83 in industry, 20 with engineering consultants)	3	18	42	24	7	3	1	1	1	100	103
Articled clerks (33 accountancy, 80 law)	87	6	5	1	—	1	—	—	—	100	113
Other appointments	6	14	33	31	10	3	1	—	2	100	665
'Other appointments' by type of employment:											
Industry	3	6	33	38	13	3	1	1	2	100	283
Commerce	9	19	34	23	8	3	1	—	3	100	116
Schools	3	15	28	34	18	2	—	—	—	100	61
Universities and technical colleges	5	19	62	5	—	5	5	—	—	100	21
Civil service	—	10	53	32	—	5	—	2	—	100	40
Local government	30	10	40	20	—	3	—	—	—	100	10
Forces	—	28	28	39	—	5	—	—	—	100	21
Agriculture	17	28	17	22	11	—	—	—	6	100	21
Other	12	28	28	20	8	3	—	—	1	100	92
All U.K. men who went directly into employment	13	14	32	27	9	3	φ	φ	2	100	881

[1] Starting salary not known for 213 men now in the United Kingdom. 44 who were overseas at the time of their first appointment, and 29 in National Service, are excluded from this table.

qualified did they start earning at the same level as those who had already been at work a few years, or did they start at a lower level because they had had less experience on the job?

If we look at earnings 4 years after graduation, it would seem that the men who had gone directly into employment after graduation had a slight advantage.

TABLE 39. *Earnings 4 years after Graduation*[1]

(Starting salary immediately after graduation is shown for comparison)

	£ per year			
	Lower quartile	Median	Upper quartile	Number of men
(i) Men who went directly into employment after graduation:				
Starting salary, first job[2]	370	440	520	744
4 years from graduation	630	740	880	807
(ii) Men who had some gap:				
4 years from graduation	570	680	780	433

[1] Excluding ministers of Religion and doctors. 4 years after graduation most of the doctors were in pre-registration hospital posts, earning under £500 p.a. Almost all the ministers of religion were also earning less than £500.

[2] Excluding articled clerks.

These figures are, however, biased by the fact that many of the men with some time-gap after graduation went into particular occupations. A good proportion were either men who took a post-graduate Diploma of Education before going into school-teaching, or Ph.D.s who went mainly into universities and non-university research posts, and the figures reflect the rates of pay in these particular occupations, not necessarily the effect of a time-gap as such. In order to discover whether, for example, the Ph.D. was worse or

TABLE 40. *Men in University and non-University Research and Development Posts: Earnings 4 years after Graduation*

	£ per year			
	Lower quartile	Median	Upper quartile	Number of men
Men with a Ph.D.	610	700	840	87
Other men	660	770	890	195

better off financially than the other graduates, we need to compare Ph.D.s and non-Ph.D.s in the same occupation groups.

There was not a great deal of difference here as the earnings of the majority of both groups came within the range £600–£900. At this early point in their careers, the Ph.D.s may have been at a slight disadvantage in comparison with those who had been longer on the job, but we cannot attach too much weight to the rather small differences, since figures of past earnings are likely to be less accurate than those for current earnings.

In general it would seem that those graduates who delayed the start of their careers were, at 4 years from graduation, likely to be earning rather less than the men who started work immediately, but this was due, at least in part, to the kind of occupation they had. Appendix III shows the current earnings of the graduates with various post-graduate qualifications; this indicates that those who did some post-graduate study, excluding the schoolteachers, were unlikely to be earning either very high salaries or very low salaries in comparison with other graduates. The point to be made here is that a post-graduate qualification such as a Ph.D. is not a means of earning a high salary, but a means of entering a particular occupation. It seems reasonable to assume that a man who wishes to become a research worker or a teacher does not consider salary to be the most important considera-tion when choosing a job.

5. Changes of employment

We have seen how the men started their careers, and what type of work they were doing in 1961. Earlier in this chapter we showed that the distribution between employment groups at the time of first appointment was very similar to the distribution at the time of the survey in 1961. The intermediate period was not static however. Between graduating and 1961 58% of the men, other than ministers of religion and doctors, had changed their employer at least once. 30% had had one change of employer, 17% two changes, 7% three changes and 4% four or more changes.*

Table 41 shows the direction of these changes. The main part of the table shows the kind of change made by those who changed employers between first appointment and the time of the survey. A number changed employers, but not their employment group; these are indicated on the table by the diagonal line of figures with the same first and current employment groups. Those who, at some time, changed their employment group as well as employer appear in the rest of the table; their first employment group being shown in the vertical columns and their current employment group in the horizontal rows. Inter-mediate changes are not shown. Table 42 summarises the main features of these move-ments, showing for each employment group the numbers who made no change, changed employer within the group, left it, or entered it. The men who went first into the Forces, the Civil Service and private legal practice tended most often to stay with the same employer. A relatively high proportion of those who started in schools, universities, accountancy practices and local government made some change, although a high proportion of the schoolteachers simply changed schools, not their type of employer. Table 42 shows also the net gain or loss of Cambridge graduates to each employment group.† More men had moved out of industry, commerce, accountancy practices, the Civil Service, local government

---

* It should be remembered that the graduates had been employed for varying lengths of time, and that some of them had therefore had more time in which to make changes. The time between graduating and starting paid employment is shown in the first part of this chapter. 70% of the men had been employed for 7 years or more at the time of the survey.

† We do not suggest, of course, that the employment groups gained or lost graduates from all universities, or that a Cambridge graduate is only replaceable by another Cambridge graduate.

TABLE 41. *Direction of Changes of Employer: First Employment Group by current Employment Group*

First appointment: Men with some change of employer

Current appointment: Men with some change of employer	Industry	Distributive trades	Insurance, banking, finance	Private practice Accountancy	Private practice Law	Other Private practices	Medicine	Church	Research establishments	Schools	Universities and technical colleges	Civil service	Local government	Journalism, art and entertainment	Agriculture	Forces	National Service	Miscellaneous	Total with change	No change	Total¹
Industry	**151**	13	16	13	6	9	3	1	8	10	14	6	2	2	3	3		3	263	252	515
Distributive trades	17	**10**	2		1					3	1	3				2			37	34	71
Insurance, banking, finance	11	4	**19**		1					3		3			1	2			53	51	104
Private practice, accounting	2	1	1	**6**		1							1						11	13	24
Private practice, law	3		4	1	**34**	1				1	3	1	1		1			2	51	74	124
Other	35	2	2	1		**29**				3	1	2	1					1	81	26	107
Medicine²	3						**84**		2	1	2		1		1		27	1	119	50	169
Church³	4							**70**	1	7	2	3							87	23	110
Research establishments	25	1	2						**7**	3	12	3	12			1		2	61	32	93
Schools	22	6	5			2		9	1	**162**	3	3	2			7			225	92	317
Universities and technical colleges	23	2				1	4	5	9	24	**57**	6	5		1	2		1	141	45	185
Civil service	2	2			2	1	1	1	1	2	3	**2**	2	2				1	19	55	74
Local government	6		2		1	3		1				3	**15**				1	1	28	4	32
Journalism, art and entertainment	6	1	1	1	1	3		1			1	2		**12**				1	30	16	46
Agriculture	3	1	3			5	4	2			2				**24**			1	41	16	57
Forces: Regular	1						4									**1**	1		9	41	50
National Service																1			5		5
Miscellaneous	6	3	2	3	2	2		2		2	1	1	2			1	1	**6**	28	9	39
Total with change	314	45	57	36	48	57	106	91	29	223	104	32	31	18	34	19	29	16	1289		
No change	252	34	51	13	74	26	50	23	32	92	45	55	4	16	16	60	29	9		833	
Total	566	79	108	49	121	83	156	114	61	315	148	87	35	34	50	60	29	27			2122

¹ Changes not known for 61 men. 13 who were temporarily unemployed at the time of the survey are excluded.

² *Medicine.* In the case of doctors, changes in the type of employment were coded, not changes of employer. For example, a move from a hospital post to general practice was recorded as a change, but a move from one hospital post to another was not.

³ *Church.* A move from one parish to another was recorded as a change, as well as a move from pastoral to some other type of employment.

In all other cases actual changes of employer were recorded. Changes are counted from the first appointment unless there was a formal training appointment; in the latter case the first appointment here means the first job after the completion of articles, pupillages or formal apprenticeships.

Note. The main part of this table shows the kind of change made by those who changed employers between their first appointment and the time of the survey. The diagonal line of bold figures shows those who changed employers, but not their employment group. Comparison of the columns (first appointment) with the horizontal rows (current appointment) shows the direction of the changes made by those who also changed their employment group.

E.g. 566 men had their first appointment in industry, and 252 of these did not change their employer. 314 had changed employers and 151 of these were still in industry at the time of the survey. 17 changed to jobs in the distributive trades, 11 to insurance, banking or finance, 2 to private practice in accountancy, 3 to private practice in law, 35 to other private practices—and so on. At the time of the survey, there were 515 men in industry, 263 of whom had some previous change of employer.

53

and the Forces than had entered these groups; more had gone into private practices other than accountancy, research institutes, universities, journalism and entertainment and agriculture than had left.

The gain to private practices was mainly at the expense of industry; research establishments also gained mainly from industry and the universities, as might be expected. The universities gained most men from industry and schools (see Table 41).

The employment groups with the highest proportion of men who made some change of employer did not necessarily contain the men who changed most often.

Table 42 shows that a high proportion of all those who went first into accountancy practices changed their employer (73%) (no doubt because accountancy is commonly regarded as an admirable prelude to a business career), but Table 43 shows that the majority changed only once. A relatively lower proportion of men who went into legal practices made any change, but those who did tended to change more often. Men entering other professional practices, commerce, agriculture and journalism had more changes than those in the Forces and research establishments.

TABLE 42. *Changes of Employer between first and current Employment Groups*

First appointment			Between first and current employment				
		No change of employer (per cent)	Change within employment group (per cent)	Left employment group (per cent)	Entered employment group Number	Net gain or loss[1]	
Employment group	Number					Number	Per cent
Industry	566	44	27	29	112	−51	−9
Distributive trades	79	43	13	44	27	−8	−10
Insurance, banking, finance	108	47	18	35	34	−4	−4
Professional practices							
Accountancy	49	27	12	61	5	−25	−51
Law	122	60	29	11	16	+3	+2
Other	83	31	35	34	52	+24	+29
Research establishments	61	53	11	36	54	+32	+52
Schools	315	29	52	19	63	+2	+1
Universities and technical colleges	149	30	39	31	83	+37	+25
Civil service	87	63	2	35	17	−13	−15
Local government	35	11	43	46	13	−3	−9
Journalism, Art and entertainment	34	47	35	18	18	+12	+35
Agriculture	50	32	48	20	17	+7	+14
Forces:	60	68	—	32	9	−10	−17
Miscellaneous	27	33	22	45	24	+12	+44
Total[2]	1825	42	29	29			

[1] Percentage of total number in the particular employment group at first appointment.

[2] This table excludes the 61 men whose changes of employer were not known, and the employment groups medicine, the Church and National Service.

TABLE 43. *Number of Changes of Employer by first Employment Group*[1]

(percentage of those with some change)

Employment group at first appointment	Number of changes of employer			Total with some change	
	I	2	3 or more	Per cent	Number
Industry	51	30	19	100	314
Commerce	44	30	26	100	102
Professional practices					
Accountancy	74	25	I	100	36
Law	47	30	23	100	48
Other	42	33	25	100	57
Research establishments	72	14	14	100	29
Schools	54	28	18	100	223
Universities and technical colleges	58	32	10	100	104
Civil service	57	31	12	100	32
Local government	60	27	13	100	31
Forces	68	32	—	100	19
Agriculture	32	34	34	100	34
Journalism, art and entertainment	29	28	43	100	18
Miscellaneous	50	28	22	100	16
Total	52	29	19	100	1065

[1] This excludes medicine, the Church and National Service.

6. Mobility and earnings

How far did the degree of mobility affect current earnings? The answer to this question must depend to some extent on the reasons the men had for changing their employer. At one end of the scale were those who were comparatively ambitious and who changed in order to better themselves financially, going to the employers who offered the highest salary; at the other end were those who had some difficulty in settling in any one occupation and did less well financially as a result. The resulting picture (Table 44) exhibits no very clear trends. There is a slight suggestion that those who moved most often tended to do less well financially, and they less often fall in the central salary range of £1500–£2000.

TABLE 44. *Current Earnings by Number of Changes of Employer*[1]

(percentage with different number of changes)

Total earnings— £ per year	Number of changes of employer				Total per cent
	0	I	2	3 or more	
Under 1000	4	6	13	10	6
1000–1499	29	39	33	40	34
1500–1999	34	34	33	26	33
2000–2999	23	16	16	20	19
3000 and over	10	5	5	3	7
Total percentage	100	100	100	100	100
Total number of men	822	647	343	200	2012

[1] This table excludes ministers of religion.

55

7. Changes in field of employment

We have so far discussed all men who changed their employer. These included a number who also changed their field of work, this type of change being defined as a major change in the direction of the graduate's career, involving a change both of employment group and type of work. 340 men had major changes of this kind (16% of the 2169 men who gave the necessary information). 96 men changed their field of work more than once, several of these returning to the field in which they first started after a period in something else. The direction of these changes was rather diverse, and showed no obvious trends between employment groups. A number of men changed from employment in industry and commerce to school or university teaching, but only a few less gave up teaching to enter industry or commerce. A few became ministers of religion after starting in secular employment. Only 3 who started their careers as ministers of religion or doctors subsequently changed the

TABLE 45. *Current Earnings by Number of Changes of Field*[1]

(percentage with different number of changes)

Total earnings: £ per year	Number of changes of field			Total per cent
	0	1	2 or more	
Under 1000	5	12	26	7
1000–1499	34	32	33	34
1500–1999	34	33	19	33
2000–2999	20	14	14	19
3000 and over	7	5	4	7
Not known	—	2	3	0
Total percentage	100	100	100	100
Total number of men	1710	242	96	2048

[1] This table excludes ministers of religion.

direction of their careers. The table below shows the distribution of current earnings for men with and without changes of field. This shows a tendency for the graduates who changed their field of work to earn less, although there were obviously some who did not appear to have suffered financially. Here, again, there were a number of different reasons for these changes. Some men were prepared to sacrifice financial gain in order to find what they felt to be more rewarding work in other respects; on the other hand there were those who changed to a field of work which seemed to offer better financial prospects than the one in which they started. Several men said that after graduation they had no clear ideas of what was entailed in different fields of work nor which would suit them best, and they took whatever job was available and seemed reasonably attractive; this did not always prove successful. It should be remembered that the men who did change the direction of their careers would have had less time to become established in their new field; it should not be assumed that they will permanently lag behind their contemporaries in their earnings.

8. Future changes

Having asked the graduates about their past and current employment, we asked, 'Can you say what you expect to be earning in 5 years' time (disregarding any effects of inflation)?' We also asked the salaried employees whether they thought this was more likely to be with the same employer, a different employer, or whether they were unable to say which was more likely.

We were interested to see if there was any relationship between the number of past changes and changes contemplated in the future, and Table 46 shows this relationship for those who answered the question about future changes.

TABLE 46. *Men working as Salaried Employees: Changes expected in 5 years' time, by previous Changes of Employer*

	Changes of employer since first appointment			
	None		One or more	
In 5 years' time	Number	Per cent	Number	Per cent
Men expecting:				
No change of employer	453	62	457	41
Some change of employer	100	14	298	26
Unable to say	173	24	380	33
Total	726	100	1135	100

Considerably more of those who had already made some change contemplated further moves, and more were uncertain where they would be in 5 years' time. This does not necessarily mean that they were unsettled; many people prefer not to remain with the same employer indefinitely, and feel that their chances of progressing are improved if they gain experience with several employers. This question did not apply to the self-employed men. The majority of these did not envisage changing the business or profession in which they were working at the time of the survey, but hoped for expansion of the business, and/or a more senior partnership with a larger share of the profits.

9. Earnings in 5 years' time

In considering what the graduates answered to this question, three points must be borne in mind.

1. The figures of future earnings are what the graduates expect (or hope for) in 5 years' time, and there may be a certain amount of wishful thinking involved in some of the answers. The results are not presented in order to try to predict what *will* happen in various fields of employment, but as a picture of what the graduates foresee for themselves.

2. 19% of the men were unable, or unwilling, to forecast their earnings in the future. The proportions varied between occupation groups, as might be expected.

There is a possibility of bias here; for example, those unable or unwilling to predict their future earnings might include an undue proportion of those who do not expect to do as well as they feel they should, although there did not appear to be any relationship between the level of current earnings and the 'unable to say' replies. The unknowns seem more related to the kind of employment; the professions, agriculture and art and entertainment all being fields where prediction is rather difficult.

TABLE 47. *Percentage of Employment Groups unable to predict Earnings in 5 years*

Current employment group	Percentage of each group 'unable to say'
Civil service and local government	8
Industry, commerce, medicine and universities	14
Schools and Forces	18
Professions other than medicine	21
Agriculture	36
Journalism, art and entertainment	38

3. Figures for future earnings were given (*a*) by those who said they intended to remain with the same employer; (*b*) by those who thought they would change; (*c*) by those who were uncertain; and (*d*) by the self-employed, to whom the question of changing employers did not apply. Most men who contemplated a change or who were uncertain commented

TABLE 48. *Basic Earnings expected in 5 years' time*

Employment group	Number of men	1961 annual earnings median: £	In 5 years' time	
			Increase median percentage[1]	Annual earnings £[2]
Industry	477	1590	45	2305
Commerce	148	1660	55	2570
Schools	266	1100	25	1370
Universities	158	1260	35	1700
Local Government	30	1430	45	2070
Civil service	67	1590	35	2150
Church	64	625	25	785
Medicine	143	1400	55	2170
Law	204	1700	65	2800
Journalism, art and entertainment	29	1540	45	2230

[1] The percentage increase was tabulated as a range of values, each group covering a 10% range; e.g. 20–29; 30–39; 40–49 etc. The mid-point only of each group is shown; the exact median may be slightly above or below this mid-point.

[2] Calculated by applying median percentage increase to the 1961 median earnings.

on their answers, and it seemed clear that very few were thinking in terms of changing their occupation or field of work. (11 of the salaried employees said they envisaged changing their field of employment.) There were no obvious differences in the percentage increases predicted as between those who contemplated a change and those who did not, or were uncertain. The figures given in Table 48 do not, therefore, distinguish the type of change envisaged.

Earnings in 5 years' time have been related to current basic earnings, i.e., for salaried employees, salary excluding any additional emoluments. We clearly could not expect any realistic estimate of future fringe benefits.

Table 48 shows the median increases expected in the main employment groups, expressed as a percentage increase on current earnings. As with current earnings, there was a fairly wide range both in terms of absolute and percentage increases, the spread being greatest in commerce and the professional practices, less in industry, and least in schools, universities, government service and the Churches. In order to complete the picture, current median earnings are shown for each employment group, and the amount in £ which would be reached if the median percentage increase is added to current earnings.

CHAPTER VI

THE MEN WORKING OVERSEAS

Completed questionnaires were received from 434 men living overseas at the time of the survey. We referred in Chapter I to the lack of definite evidence of the citizenship of some of these men, and to the difficulty in distinguishing between those who were working in a business or profession not connected with the United Kingdom, and those whose employer was in the United Kingdom. Because of these difficulties, and in view of the rather small uumbers working in any one country and in any one occupation, we have treated the overseas men as a single group. In the preceding three chapters this information from the men working in the United Kingdom is presented in some detail; in this chapter we do not give as much detail, the aim being to outline the main differences in overseas employment.

1. Place of work and nationality

85 of the men overseas were foreign or Commonwealth nationals who returned to their country of origin after completing their education in the United Kingdom. 7 were foreign nationals working outside their own countries. The remaining 340 men were British nationals, probably mostly of United Kingdom origin, but some possibly citizens of other Commonwealth countries either by birth or by naturalisation. Table 49 shows where these men were living at the time of the survey.

The men shown as 'other British' nationals in Table 49 included 17 from the United Kingdom who had definitely emigrated to Canada, and 17 who appeared to have settled in Canada but gave no definite evidence on this point. 26 men from the United Kingdom appeared to have settled in the United States, and 28 were probably permanently resident in various other countries.

The time the men had spent overseas was not necessarily an indication of the permanence of their residence outside the United Kingdom; some who had spent all their working time since graduation overseas clearly intended to return eventually; others had only recently left the United Kingdom but intended to settle overseas. Table 50 shows how long the men had been working overseas since graduation.

2. Type of employment

The largest employment groups were industry, education and government service. The majority of the men in civil government service were United Kingdom citizens in the Overseas Civil Service in Commonwealth territories, nearly half of them in Africa. Table 51 shows the main employment groups in various countries.

Most of the men in universities were in the United States, Africa or Australia, and most of those in schools and education departments were in Africa. The ministers of religion were mainly in Africa.

TABLE 49. *Men working Overseas: Place of Work by Nationality*[1]

Place of work

Nationality	Australia	Canada	India and Pakistan	S. & N. Rhodesia	Kenya	South Africa	Other African	Other Commonwealth	U.S.A.	Europe	Other Foreign	Total
Foreign — in their country of origin	—	9	—	—	—	10	3	—	12	5	1	31
Commonwealth — of origin	13	12	6	—	—	—	—	14	—	—	—	54
Other foreign	1	—	—	—	1	—	—	—	—	—	5	7
Other British	12	45	10	5	25	9	72	54	48	33	27	340
Total	22	58	22	11	26	19	75	68	60	38	33	432

[1] Place of work not known for 2 men.

TABLE 50. *Time overseas since Graduation, by Place of Work*

Time overseas[1]	Place of work in 1961								Total
	Australia	Canada	India and Pakistan	All African territories	Other Commonwealth	U.S.A.	Europe	Other Foreign	
Under 1 year	1	2	1	2	3	6	4	—	19
1–3 years	4	6	—	20	15	9	6	4	64
3–5 years	5	11	6	22	10	12	8	4	78
Over 5 years[2]	3	12	2	19	13	5	7	8	69
Since graduation	9	23	12	57	19	25	8	13	166
Not known	—	4	1	11	8	3	5	4	36
Total	22	58	22	131	68	60	38	33	432

[1] Total time since graduation, not necessarily consecutive.
[2] Over 5 years, but not the whole time since graduation.

TABLE 51. *Employment Group by Place of Work*[1]

Employment group	Place of work								Total	
	Australia	Canada	India and Pakistan	Africa	Other Commonwealth	U.S.A.	Europe	Other foreign	Number	Percentage
Civil government service	—	7	5	38	14	4	6	5	79	19
Forces	1	—	—	2	7	—	3	1	14	3
Education:										
Universities[2]	9	7	2	11	4	23	—	2	58	14
Schools[2]	3	4	—	18	1	2	1	2	31	7
Industry	2	15	7	15	17	15	8	9	88	20
Commerce:										
Insurance, banking and finance	3	4	1	5	5	2	3	7	30	7
Distributive trades	—	2	1	8	5	1	4	3	24	6
Church	1	2	3	19	2	1	2	1	31	7
Medicine	1	9	1	1	6	4	—	—	21	5
Law: private practice	—	1	1	3	3	1	—	—	9	2
Other private practice[3]	1	5	1	4	2	4	3	—	20	5
Agriculture	1	1	—	4	1	—	1	2	10	2
Journalism, art and entertainment	—	1	—	—	1	2	3	—	7	2
Miscellaneous	—	—	1	1	—	1	2	1	6	1
Total	22	58	22	129	68	60	36	33	428	100

[1] This table excludes 6 men temporarily unemployed or engaged in full-time study.
[2] Includes those working in education departments, not necessarily teaching.
[3] Mainly civil engineering consultants.

14 of the 428 men shown in Table 51 were employed in a family business in industry or commerce. 34 were self-employed; 8 of these in agriculture, 8 in law, 9 in medicine, 2 in industry and commerce and 8 in other employment groups. The remaining 380 men were salaried employees in non-family concerns.

Table 51 includes but does not distinguish the 85 graduates of foreign and Commonwealth nationality who returned to their own countries after graduating. These were scattered through all the employment groups; 30 were in industry or commerce, 10 in universities, 6 in schools, 14 in government service, 8 in agriculture, 17 in other groups. They include 12 of the 14 men employed in a family business.

3. Qualifications

There was little evidence that overseas employment attracted any special kind of graduate so far as academic qualifications were concerned. A slightly higher proportion of the men

TABLE 52. *Degree Subject*

	Percentage of men overseas	Percentage of men in the United Kingdom
Agriculture, estate management, architecture	5	5
Engineering	8	11
Science and mathematics	27	31
Arts	60	53
Total	100	100

working overseas were arts graduates—60% as against 53% of the men in the United Kingdom, and a correspondingly lower proportion had read engineering, science and mathematics.

There is some discussion nowadays about the number of graduates with good academic qualifications, particularly scientists and engineers, who are attracted to overseas employment, and are lost to the United Kingdom. So far as this group of Cambridge graduates is concerned, the numbers did not seem to be very great—434 of the men who completed questionnaires were overseas at the time of the survey, i.e. 16% of the whole sample. This includes the 85 men of Commonwealth and foreign nationality who returned to their own countries. Of the remaining 349 men, 89 were in the Overseas Civil Service or the Foreign Office, or working in the education departments of Commonwealth territories. It was not always possible to tell from the questionnaires whether the men in industry and commerce were employed by firms based in the United Kingdom but the minimum number employed in this way was 30 men.

Excluding the 31 ministers of religion working in various capacities for the Church, this leaves 199 men of United Kingdom nationality who were not known to be working for an organisation based in the United Kingdom. A number of these had emigrated to Canada

TABLE 53. *Total Earnings by Place of Work*

(Excluding 6 men unemployed)

Total earnings £ per year[1]	Place of work									Total
	Australia	Canada	India and Pakistan	South Africa	Other African	Other Commonwealth	U.S.A.	Europe	Other foreign	
Under 1000	1	1	7	—	15	5	1	3	1	34
1000–1499	3	5	5	3	6	6	3	5	1	37
1500–1999	7	5	—	7	18	10	6	7	3	63
2000–2499	6	4	1	1	33	12	—	7	3	67
2500–2999	1	11	—	5	18	12	11	5	5	68
3000–3999	1	19	4	—	13	16	16	1	7	77
4000–4999	2	4	4	1	1	4	12	2	4	34
5000–9999	1	5	—	2	4	2	11	6	4	35
10,000 and over	—	1	—	—	—	—	—	—	1	2
Not known	—	3	1	—	2	1	—	—	4	11
Total	22	58	22	19	110	68	60	36	33	428

[1] Basic salary plus allowances and additional emoluments. All overseas currencies converted to £ sterling at 1961 rates of exchange.

5

or the U.S.A. since they graduated but we could not always distinguish those who intended to remain overseas from those who intended to return to the United Kingdom at some time. Approximately 50 men seemed to be fairly settled in the U.S.A., or Canada, and 26 in other countries, at least for the immediate future.

Examining the qualifications of these 199 men who may be 'lost 'to the United Kingdom, at least temporarily, we find that 73 of them were scientists or engineers, 25 of these in the U.S.A. and 20 in Canada. 9 of them had obtained a First Class Honours degree, and 29 had a Ph.D. (17 of the Ph.D.s were in the U.S.A., all but 2 in university posts). This is 15% of all those in the sample who had a Ph.D. Even if non-response from graduates living overseas was higher than from those in the United Kingdom, and what little evidence we have suggests that the reverse may be the case, these figures do not suggest that there was a disproportionate loss to the United Kingdom of the best of this generation of Cambridge graduates.

4. Earnings

The variations in the cost of living in different countries makes any detailed comparison of earnings difficult. Men employed in the Forces, the Overseas Civil Service and the Foreign Office, and in industrial and commercial concerns based in the United Kingdom, all had overseas allowances adjusted to the cost of living in the countries in which they were working. The rates of pay of those working in other professions or businesses tend to reflect conditions within the particular countries as well as occupational rates. There were some general trends however. Ministers of religion in all the territories received lower pay than those in other occupations. Men in industry and commerce tended to earn more than those in education or government service in most territories. Expatriate civil servants (i.e. United Kingdom nationals serving overseas) mostly had considerably higher pay and allowances than civil servants who were nationals of the country concerned. Table 53 shows the range of earnings in the various territories.

Most of those earning less than £1000 were unpaid members of religious communities or employed by one of the religious denominations. 3 were Commonwealth nationals working as civil servants in their own countries.

The United Kingdom nationals employed in the Overseas Civil Service were mostly earning between £2000 and £3999, depending on the country they were in. Most of those earning over £5000 were in industry or commerce, but 3 were in Government service, 5 in agriculture, and 1 in medicine. Most of the men in university posts were earning between £2000 and £2999; 4 were earning over £3000 (in the U.S.A.).

CHAPTER VII

THE WOMEN GRADUATES

The object of the women's questionnaire was twofold. First, to assess the current employment position of women in their early thirties. The age group chosen was the same as for the men, and for similar reasons (see Chapter I), but there are of course factors to be considered in the case of the women which do not affect the men so directly: namely those domestic responsibilities which are usually the women's concern, whether these consist of running a home for husband and children, or the care of parents or other dependants.

The second aim of the survey was to investigate the extent to which older women were available for work, with particular emphasis on those who might consider returning to work after a period occupied with domestic responsibilities, and for this purpose we chose the graduates of 1937 and 1938. In this section of the report we consider first the position of the women who were in paid employment at the time of the survey, and we later discuss the question of the availability of women graduates for work.

It should be said at the outset that we do not wish to imply any judgments about the desirability or otherwise of women working in paid employment. We are aware that for some women the job of looking after a family is their prime interest, and they may require no other, and that it is perfectly possible to be a useful and contented member of society without having paid employment. If in what follows there seems to be undue emphasis on those who are now working or wish to return to work, this is simply because our task is to discover what the potential labour force is. A further point that should be made is that we use the words 'occupied' and 'working' as a convenient way of referring to graduates working in paid employment as distinct from those occupied solely with domestic tasks and voluntary work; the latter can, of course, be more time consuming and can entail more hard work than a regular paid job.

1. The general background

The graduates' general background and qualifications are discussed in Chapter II. The main features are as follows:

1937/1938 graduates. 9% came up to Cambridge having already taken a degree at another university. 62% read for an arts degree, and 37% for a degree in science or mathematics. 21% obtained a post-graduate Diploma in Education, 6% obtained other 1-year post-graduate diplomas, 7% post-graduate diplomas or degrees requiring 2 years of study. 4% obtained a Ph.D. and 9% qualified as doctors.

1952/1953 graduates. 4% came up having already obtained a degree at another university. 61% read for an arts degree and 37% for a degree in science or mathematics. Only one woman took a degree in engineering. 20% obtained a post-graduate Diploma of Education,

67

6% other 1-year diplomas (several of these in social studies), 4% completed 2-year post-graduate courses, 9% obtained a Ph.D., 8% qualified as doctors, and 1% obtained legal qualifications.

To complete this brief survey of the background, Table 54 shows what the women did immediately after graduation, and indicates the time spent in the various activities. 37% of the older women graduates continued with some form of full-time study, 44% of the younger group. 46% of the older graduates and 43% of the younger went immediately into a full-time job. Among those who had no immediate job are included those in both groups who never worked at all after graduation; 7 women of the 1937/1938 group and 8 in the 1952/1953.

TABLE 54. *First Activity after Graduation*

Activity		Time spent—years[1]					Total	
		Up to 1	1–2	2–3	Over 3	Not known	Number	Percentage of each age group
Full-time study	1937–38	51	5	11	10	—	77	37
	1952–53	71	11	33	9	—	124	44
Full-time job	1937–38	8	6	1	82	—	97	46
	1952–53	21	14	12	71	—	118	43
Part-time job	1937–38	4	1	—	—	—	5	2
	1952–53	7	—	—	1	—	8	3
No job	1937–38	2	5	2	14	—	23	11
	1952–53	12	5	1	10	—	28	10
Not known	1937–38	—	—	—	—	8	8	4
	1952–53	—	—	—	—	6	6	2

[1] The time spent in the particular activity before a change of some kind. E.g. 21 graduates of 1952/1953 went into full-time employment immediately after graduation, continued this for up to a year, then gave up full-time work for a period. They were not necessarily continuously unoccupied after this, and some later came back to work. Similarly, 12 graduates of 1952/1953 had no job for up to 1 year after graduation, and then found full- or part-time work.

2. Continuity of work

Tables 55 and 56 show the total time spent in paid employment since graduation.

It is now 24 or 25 years since the 1937/1938 group graduated, so they have had more scope for changes to occur. Only 55 of the 84 now in full-time employment have worked continuously since graduating. Of those now in part time employment, only 6 have worked continuously while 32 have had periods of unemployment. The periods away from work were mainly spent in bringing up a family, the current occupation for most of the un-employed graduates of 1952/1953. Most of these took up work immediately after graduation and have since stopped. The majority of the graduates of the 1952/1953 group now in full time employment have worked continuously since graduation; these are mostly single women. Those in part time work at present are almost all married, and have spent a longer time unoccupied.

TABLE 55. *1937/1938 Graduates: Time in Paid Employment since Graduation*

Continuity of work	Total years in paid employment since graduation				Total
Now in full-time employment	1–5	6–10	11–20	21–25	
Worked continuously since graduation	—	—	—	55	55
Some time unoccupied since graduation[1]	—	5	20	4	29
Total employed full time	—	5	20	59	84
Percentage of all employed full time	—	6	24	70	100
Now in part-time employment					
Worked continuously since graduation	—	—	1	5	6
Some time unoccupied since graduation[1]	5	11	16	—	32
Total employed part time	5	11	17	5	38
Percentage of all employed part time	13	29	45	13	100
Now unoccupied					
Some time in work since graduation[2]	23	34	14	—	71
No paid work since graduation	—	—	—	—	7
Total number unoccupied	23	34	14	—	78
Percentage of all unoccupied	29	44	18	—	100

[1] The majority of these did some work immediately after graduation, subsequently had an unoccupied period, and have since returned to work.

[2] The majority of these did some work immediately after graduation, and have since been unoccupied. These figures do not include 10 who either did not answer the question or who did not remember some of the facts.

TABLE 56. *1952/1953 Graduates: Time in Paid Employment since Graduation*

Continuity of work[1]	Total years in paid employment since graduation				Total
Now in full-time employment	1–3	4–5	6–7	8–9	
Worked continuosuly since graduation	1	11	23	47	82
Some time unoccupied since graduation	2	7	5	4	18
Total employed full-time	3	18	28	51	100
Percentage of all employed full time	3	18	28	51	100
Now in part-time employment					
Worked continuously since graduation	—	5	3	7	15
Some time unoccupied since graduation	5	8	13	1	27
Total employed part time	5	13	16	8	42
Percentage of all employed part time	12	31	38	19	100
Now unoccupied					
Some time in work since graduation[2]	60	41	19	6	126
No paid work since graduation	—	—	—	—	8
Total number unoccupied	60	41	19	6	134
Percentage of all unoccupied	45	31	14	4	100

[1] In Tables 55 and 56 periods of 'work' include both full-time study and paid employment. Therefore a 1953 graduate who did 3 years of post-graduate full-time study and has since been in a paid job, will have 'worked' continuously, with 5 years of paid employment.

[2] Almost all of these 126 graduates started work immediately after graduation, and subsequently gave up their paid employment.

The table excludes 8 who either did not answer the question or who did not remember some of the facts.

3. The women living overseas

27 of the 1937/1938 graduates who completed questionnaires were living overseas at the time of the survey, and 57 of the 1952/1953 graduates. We unfortunately did not ask questions which enabled us to be sure how many were permanently abroad, and how many only temporarily. It seemed, however, that many of the factors affecting the amount and kind of employment the graduates were doing, or wished to do in the future, were the same for those overseas and those in the United Kingdom, and in view of the small numbers in the groups concerned we have not usually presented the information from the women living overseas separately.

Of the 27 1937/1938 graduates living overseas, 10 were working at the time of the survey; 4 of these were probably permanently resident abroad. 17 were unoccupied, 11 of these were probably permanently overseas. Of the 57 1952/1953 graduates living overseas, 31 were working, 11 of these probably permanently abroad, and 26 were unoccupied, 9 of these probably permanently overseas.

4. Employment status

Table 57 shows the employment status of the women at the time of the survey. Not surprisingly, the majority of single women were working full time, and they accounted for some two-thirds of all those in each age group who were doing so. 43% of the 1937/1938 married women were in paid employment of some kind, but only 35% of the 1952/1953 married women.

TABLE 57. *Marital Status by Employment Status: Women living in the United Kingdom and Overseas*

	1937–1938				1952–1953			
Employment status[1]	Single	Married	Widowed or divorced	Total	Single	Married	Widowed or divorced	Total
Working full time	58	22	9	89	71	28	4	103
Part time between 21 and 30 hours per week	2	6	1	9	—	6	—	6
Part time between 11 and 20 hours per week	—	16	1	17	—	15	—	15
Part time, 10 hours per week or less	—	14	2	16	2	21	1	24
Unoccupied	2	75	2	79	4	132	—	136
Total	62	133	15	210	77	202	5	284

[1] The 1937/1938 graduates include: 2 self-employed working full time
2 self-employed working 11–20 hours a week
5 self-employed working 10 hours or less a week
The 1952/1953 graduates include: 2 self-employed working full time
2 self-employed working 21–30 hours a week
3 self-employed working 11–20 hours a week
7 self-employed working 10 hours or less a week

TABLE 58. *Type of Work of all Graduates in Paid Employment by Degree Subject: United Kingdom and Overseas (Full- and Part-time)*

Present job	1937-1938					1952-1953				
	Science	Mathematics	Arts	Total Number	Total Percentage	Science	Mathematics	Arts	Total Number	Total Percentage
School-teaching	15	14	29	58	44	11	3	22	36	24
Universities and technical college teaching	1	2	14	17	13	9	5	16	30	20
Other university posts	1	—	2	3	2	—	—	1	1	1
Doctors	10	—	1	11	8	16	—	—	16	11
Other hospital posts	2	—	4	6	5	2	2	5	9	6
Industry	1	—	—	1	1					
Government and local government service	1	2	12	15	11	1	1	13	15	10
Other professional services	1	—	5	6	5	—	—	3	3	2
Other employed	4	1	9	14	11	7	1	29	37	25
Other self-employed	—	—	—	—	—	—	—	1	1	1
Total	36	19	76	131	100	46	12	90	148	100

5. The working women

Type of work. Table 58 shows the type of work the women were doing at the time of the survey.

A high proportion of both groups were teaching in schools or universities: well over half the older graduates, and rather less than half the younger women. Government service took second place with the older women; 2 were local authority youth officers, the remainder in various civil service posts. Medicine took third place, with 11 graduates. Only one was in industry, occupied in research.

The figures for the 1952/1953 graduates show a greater diversity of occupations, with a few more in industrial posts and a considerably lower proportion of schoolteachers. The rather large number included under 'other employed' include such jobs as secretarial and clerical posts, librarians, writers and editors, school matrons, social workers, and members of religious communities.

6. Earnings

Table 59 shows the distribution of earnings for the women working in the United Kingdom. Those working overseas are excluded because of the difficulty of equating the different costs of living. The figures are total earnings, i.e. basic salary plus any additional emoluments. Most of the women in full-time work belonged to a superannuation scheme, and 24 of them had other benefits ranging in value from £20 to £300. Very few of the women in part-time work had additional emoluments of any kind. The hours of part-time work were very variable, and we have not related earnings to hours of work apart from showing those in full-time work separately. Only 3 women working less than 10 hours a week were earning more than £300; these were all earning under £400.

As might be expected, it was mainly the older graduates who had reached the higher grade teaching and civil service posts or were earning more as doctors. Out of the 15 with total earnings of over £2000, 4 were earning between £2500 and £2999, 3 between £3000 and £3999, and 1 over £4000. Three of the younger graduates were earning over £2000, but none had reached £2500. It is perhaps surprising that although many of the older graduates had been in full-time work at least twice as long as the younger women, there was not more difference in their earnings. This is to a large extent a reflection of the fact that so many of both age groups were in school-teaching, where there are relatively few posts of any kind which carry salaries of over £2000.

7. Satisfaction

The women graduates were asked to allocate scores to a list of possible sources of satisfaction or dissatisfaction in their work, in the same way as the men (see Chapter IV), and the total score was calculated as a percentage of the maximum. As we said in Chapter IV, this method of scoring is used to contrast the obviously dissatisfied with the obviously satisfied, and we do not feel there is any value in attempting to interpret differences in the rather wide range of 'just satisfied' to 'moderately satisfied' scores. The figures in Table 60

TABLE 59. *Total Earnings by Type of Work: United Kingdom Women only*[1]

Type of employment	Year	Part-time work			Annual Earnings: £ per year												Total
		Under 150	150–299	300–499	500–749 Full time	500–749 Part time	750–999 Full time	750–999 Part time	1000–1499 Full time	1000–1499 Part time	1500–1999 Full time	1500–1999 Part time	2000 and over Full time	Not known Full time	Not known Part time	
School-teaching	37/38	—	7	8	—	1	5	1	21	—	5	—	5	—	2	55
	52/53	1	1	2	—	2	2	—	16	—	1	—	—	2	1	28
University and technical college posts	37/38	1	—	2	1	—	1	—	6	1	6	—	2	—	—	20
	52/53	3	3	1	—	1	2	—	9	1	1	—	—	—	—	21
Medicine and other hospital posts	37/38	1	2	2	—	2	2	1	—	—	1	2	4	—	—	17
	52/53	—	1	2	—	2	—	1	6	1	1	—	—	—	—	14
Industrial research, production and personnel work	37/38	—	—	—	—	—	—	—	—	—	1	—	—	—	—	1
	52/53	—	—	—	—	—	1	—	5	—	3	—	—	—	—	9
Civil service and local government	37/38	—	1	—	—	—	—	—	2	—	7	—	4	—	—	14
	52/53	—	—	—	—	—	3	—	3	—	—	—	3	—	—	9
Other professional practices	37/38	1	—	—	1	—	1	—	—	—	—	—	—	—	—	3
	52/53	—	—	—	—	—	1	—	1	—	1	—	—	—	—	3
All other posts	37/38	3	2	—	3	—	—	—	1	—	—	—	—	—	2	11
	52/53	7	3	—	5	1	4	—	6	—	1	—	—	—	4	31
Total 1937/1938		6	12	12	5	3	9	2	30	1	20	2	15	—	4	121
Total 1952/1953		11	8	5	5	6	13	1	46	2	8	—	3	2	5	115

[1] This table excludes two members of religious communities.

show the scores for the two groups of women. (Excluding those who did not answer the question.)

There were no obvious differences between those in different occupations, but the numbers in occupations other than teaching were too small for any conclusions to be reached on this point. The scores suggest that more of the older women graduates were satisfied with their general conditions of work and fewer dissatisfied than the younger women; this is in agreement with the general impression given by the comments on the questionnaires. Comparing the overall scores of the women with those of the men (Chapter IV), it would seem that the women were more often satisfied and less often dissatisfied than the men. There are several possible reasons for this, one being that the women more often look to

TABLE 60. *Satisfaction Scores*

(percentage of each group)

	Dissatisfied 0–24	25–74	Satisfied 75–100	Total	Number in group
1937/38 Full time work	3	50	47	100	80
1937/38 Part time work	6	49	45	100	41
1952/53 Full time work	12	48	40	100	80
1952/53 Part time work	9	52	39	100	37

their family life to provide satisfaction and expect less from their work, and so are less often disappointed in their work.

Very few of the women expressed dissatisfaction with their pay. 5 of the 1937/1938 graduates working full time were dissatisfied; 3 of those working part time. 8 of the younger graduates working full time and 4 of those working part time were dissatisfied. The majority of both age groups were either moderately or entirely satisfied, or had no particular feelings on the subject (or did not care to express them).

8. Prospects and suitability of work

We asked the graduates to comment on their own prospects and their experience of the general availability of suitable work for women graduates. We also asked those who cared to do so to comment on the status of women in their own field as compared with men. While we realise that answers to these questions must be largely subjective, we feel that these are matters of considerable interest to most working women, and that a summary of the graduates' views are of value in indicating some of the factors these women have found to be important, and in indicating their own attitude to their work.

The range of jobs open to women graduates is less than that for men, although the position has been improving over the years, and will continue to improve. The reasons why this should be so are complex, and often interrelated. The question of the suitability of jobs for women cannot be dissociated from the fact that married women with children, or any women with domestic responsibilities, have special problems. This is perhaps too obvious to need much comment, but is sometimes forgotten in the course of general discussions about the availability of work for women graduates.

There are obviously several fields of work in which a married woman is at a disadvantage. Jobs requiring long and irregular hours or much travelling are often out of the question, so are those which require residence on the job. The choice of employment for a married woman is often limited by the fact that her husband's job may necessitate moving, which means that she cannot commit herself to long-term employment. There is also the question of whether she has the physical energy to cope with both domestic demands and outside work, and how far she can relegate home responsibilities to the back of her mind, particularly if the work is intellectually very demanding. Most of the married women who answered the questionnaire were aware of these difficulties. One graduate who continued her successful professional career after marriage said that her 'ambition to get to the top had much diminished since marriage' and she had 'acquired a new scale of priorities'. She went on to say that 'this may be what employers sense when they are traditionally cautious of employing a woman on a long-term basis'.

Apart from the problem of domestic responsibilities, there is the question of how far women are affected by discrimination on grounds of sex alone. Here, there is a good deal of variation. In the teaching profession, both schools and universities, and in the civil service, women and men have equal status. This is by no means general in industry and commerce. There are some employers who prefer not to employ women at all; some who pay lip service to the principal of equal status and opportunities for men and women, but in practice confine their recruitment of women to certain limited fields of work; and others again who genuinely make no discrimination and treat all their employees on their individual merits. Where discrimination against women does exist, it is not necessarily on the grounds of sex alone; some employers are reluctant to engage single women who may leave in a short time to get married, or reluctant to employ a married woman whose energies and interests may be divided between her home and her work. Some women themselves said that they had little desire for posts of responsibility, although this is not an exclusively feminine attitude. On the other hand, there are many women who would welcome responsibility, but find that it is not readily offered to them unless they are of 'much more than average ability'. Some women feel that men dislike the idea of working under a woman. This may well be so. One woman said that her husband worked for a large industrial firm which, in practice, does not employ women graduates; this, her husband was told, was 'not by directive but as a result of the sheer embarrassment felt at the prospect of women in a managerial relation to men'.

Having said that women graduates often have particular problems to face in finding suitable work, it should also be said that there were a number who did not feel that any problems existed; there always have been, and will continue to be, women who have the ability to combine domestic responsibilities and a successful working career without detriment to either. None the less, any report on the kind of employment undertaken by women graduates raises the question of why they are so often found in some fields of employment, and so rarely in others. For an easier appraisal of the employment situation as seen by graduates of both age groups, the main types of work are discussed below under separate headings.

School-teaching. 'Teaching is obviously very satisfying if one has taken up the right career.' This comment expresses what many of the graduates felt, and there were few who appeared to think they had taken up the wrong career. Several had entered school-teaching with some apprehension initially because they had been unable to find suitable posts elsewhere, but most of these had found the work rewarding and did not regret their decision. There are also obvious advantages to women with domestic responsibilities in that the work fits more or less easily into the routine of running a home with children at school. There is clearly plenty of scope for women science teachers, and owing to the shortage of scientists a number of women with mathematics degrees had been co-opted to teach physics. The shortage of teachers often enables a graduate to obtain a post without having taken a teachers' training course, which has been an advantage to some of the married women who could not have afforded the time for a full training course.

Most single women felt the outlook to be reasonably good, although it was said that there was a preference for the appointment of men to the more senior posts when the schools are co-educational. One of the 1937/1938 graduates thought that the long-term prospects of headship were becoming less bright, since the building of large new schools, grouping smaller schools together, would reduce the number of headships available.

There seemed to be little difference in the scope and outlook of married and single women teachers except that for the married, residential posts are usually impossible and headships more difficult to obtain. There was evidently reluctance on the part of some education authorities to offer permanent posts to married women, although there were plenty of temporary posts available.

A few of the older women expressed themselves fairly strongly on the general attitude to education, which, as one graduate said, 'is not valued, nor is a teacher's worth regarded as of any real importance, except by a tiny minority'. The younger graduates tended to be rather more optimistic and to feel that the importance of education was becoming more generally recognised.

University, training college and technical college teaching. The prospects in these fields for women graduates were generally considered good but some felt that they could not hope to achieve the degree of promotion reached by men, and pointed out that there are women professors in the arts, but relatively few in science or mathematics. Women nominally have equal status with men in university teaching, and although some of the older graduates felt that there was discrimination against women in making initial appointments, fewer of the younger women seemed to feel this was so. One of the younger graduates gave it as her opinion that 'instances of women as such failing to obtain employment, working facilities or promotion in universities date from the inter-war period or earlier, and would not occur today'. It was thought that in technical colleges there is some prejudice against women lecturers, and that promotion among the female staff was slow. While there would seem to be no difference in scope between single and married women, provided there are no young children, technical colleges were said to prefer single women on the whole. Where libraries are concerned, the prospects for men and women are equal, although the top posts are more often held by men.

The Civil Service. Long term prospects for the woman graduate are good, especially for the single women, more especially in the administrative grade. The proportion of women to men in the scientific grades is very small, especially among the older women.

There is equal pay and almost all posts are interchangeable between men and women. A woman can reach the top positions, but it was said that she had, generally speaking, to be of a higher standard than a man to reach an equivalent position, and senior posts in the scientific civil service are in practice rarely held by women. There is no marriage bar, but married women cannot be so mobile and so their scope is more limited. There was thought to be considerably less prejudice against the married woman in the civil service than outside it; indeed, most women now employed in the service commented on the lack of prejudice and the opportunities to be found therein.

In so far as the administrative grade of the civil service is concerned, there are no part-time posts, and so far (1961) no re-entry of women who resigned on marriage, although direct recruitment of entrants over 30 as principals has lately been introduced. One of the younger women felt that too many graduates assumed that a career in the civil service necessarily meant the administrative grades or the Foreign Office, whereas there were also possibilities in the executive grades and in various specialist branches.

There were a few women who had had posts in the overseas civil service, and found the work immensely rewarding and the conditions of employment good. They suggested that there was ample scope for satisfying a desire for adventure, interest, and usefulness in a variety of fields, particularly in teaching, agriculture and medicine. One woman commented that graduates with less than a 2.i Honours degree were often discouraged from applying for posts in the overseas civil service, but that she had found that graduates with a 2.ii or Third Class Honours were recruited.

Factory Inspectorate Branch of the Civil Service. There were said to be very good prospects here for the single woman, particularly for those with scientific qualifications. There is no difference at all in status between men and women, and women can and do reach the higher grades. Although there is no marriage bar, there is less scope for the married woman because of the liability to transfer both during training and normal service, particularly on promotion.

Medicine: Hospital work. For the more junior posts there is no difference in pay, status, or duties between men and women; it was said, however, that there are proportionately fewer women in hospitals with permanent staff appointments, and that, given equal qualifications, a man would almost always be chosen. It was said to be rather hard for women to get senior jobs, and one of the older women commented that 'the discrimination is subtle, but was strong in my generation'. A younger (married) graduate, commenting on the keen competition for first-rate hospital posts, said that few married women doctors felt able to compete, and that 'if they do take up such work, home responsibilities have to be kept strictly out of the day's work'.

Hospital administration was said to offer few openings for women, but it was thought that in view of the expected expansion of the hospital service the prospects would improve in the future.

General practice and public health. Full-time work, for the married or single woman doctor, is available both in general practice and public health departments; with excellent opportunities owing to the shortage of trained men and women for posts of this nature. There is no difference in scope and status between men and women in public health and local authority work.

Dietetics. There is an acute shortage of trained staff for hospital work and so it follows that there will be both full and part-time work available in this profession for some time to come.

Almoners. One of the younger women expressed surprise that so few Cambridge graduates entered this profession, which she had found extremely satisfying and interesting. There were said to be many vacant posts, both full- and part-time in case work, teaching, administration and sociological research in hospitals and also in local authority departments. The rate of pay, though formerly rather low, has now been somewhat improved, and the recognition given to qualified social workers by the Younghusband report was said to have "great implications."

Social work in general is one of the types of employment where more women are employed than men. It is, however, rather difficult for the married woman to obtain employment unless she can give a considerable amount of time, as there is often much evening and weekend work entailed which she is usually less able to undertake than the single woman.

Industry. Some of the rather few women engaged in industry in various capacities were bitter about the lack of status, pay and prospects compared with those for men. In some companies, it was said, there are men earning 2–3 times as much as women similarly employed. One graduate continued, women 'are considered not to have careers; their function is to provide well qualified cheap labour'. Two women quoted instance of jobs of similar content and status, which were 'graded' as 'male jobs', and women paid at the rate of 80% of the equivalent mens' salary. It was said that if a woman succeeded a man in a certain job, the post was usually downgraded. Another woman gave as an example of a less important, but irritating, type of discrimination, the fact that in her firm leave allocation is different for men; men are given $20\frac{1}{2}$ days leave after 5 years service, women after 8 years.

One woman chemist engaged in industrial research, directing a small team of research workers, stated that she found no difference in scope between single and married women and men, but that women had no prospects of management posts. Women graduate chemists, engineers and mathematicians engaged in industry are limited by the fact that no woman is appointed as plant or works manager, an experience necessary to most men graduates before they proceed to more responsible technical administrative posts. A woman factory inspector considered that there are far greater possibilities in industry both in research and management for men, and so women with technical qualifications tend to go more often into the factory inspectorate where there is equality of pay and opportunity. On the credit side, there was said to be less discrimination against women in research establishments, with, usually, equality of pay and status. There was also said to be openings for women on the personnel side in industry, and sometimes in advertising. One of the younger graduates, working for an advertising agency, said that this was one of the fields where women were at no disadvantage compared with men.

Secretarial work. Several graduates had taken secretarial courses after graduation, and had found interesting jobs as a result. One of these graduates, however, said that she doubted the wisdom of taking such a course, since she felt that once the label 'secretary' was attached, it was rare for a woman to obtain promotion to an executive position. She felt that it was important for a graduate who did obtain a secretarial training to ensure that she became really proficient in shorthand, and did not rely simply on being a graduate. She thought that some graduates tended to despise slightly their secretarial qualifications, and were not always welcomed by business firms as a result.

Law. This is a field which comparatively few women enter at present, but in which they seem to feel at no disadvantage. One practising solicitor said she had met with no discrimination, but pointed out the, perhaps obvious, fact that law is not a career for a woman who wants a stop-gap job or a quiet life.

In this rather general summary of the views most commonly expressed by the women who completed questionnaires, the question of competition between men and women is a recurrent theme. This is because it was obviously felt to be important by so many of the graduates. The reason why so many women are, or feel themselves to be at a disadvantage compared with men is clearly a many-sided question, but clearly relevant to any discussion of the availability of women graduates for work.

9. The unoccupied women

79 of the 1937/1938 graduates and 136 of the 1952/1953 graduates were not in paid employment at the time of the survey. The majority of both groups said that their reason for not working was that they were too fully occupied with domestic responsibilities. Several said they had no financial need to work, a few said they had no desire to. 5 were unable to work because of ill-health, and 2 were engaged in full-time study. 7 said they were unable to find suitable jobs (4 of these were overseas), and 2 were temporarily unemployed, between jobs.

These graduates were asked if they wished to take up paid work in the future, and, if so, when this might be, and what type of work they would like to do. Table 61 shows how many envisaged being available for work, and how soon.

The majority of those wishing to return to work full time envisaged doing so when their children had finished their schooling; those who contemplated part-time work usually said that it should not be during school holidays, or out of school hours.

The majority of those in both age groups who wished to return to work at some time stated their preference for part-time work. A higher proportion of the older women had no wish to return to work at all; it may be that more of the younger graduates will have similar feelings when they reach the same age; several of them said they found it difficult to envisage their circumstances or their feelings in 5 to 10 years time.

Table 62 shows the main types of employment these graduates were last in, and the most commonly expressed preferences for work in the future. A number in both groups said that they did not mind what kind of work they did next, provided it was interesting. The miscellaneous preferences included scientific research, market research, archaeology, translation work, and research into historical records and anthropology. The majority of both

TABLE 61. *Graduates not working at present*

Time when available	Within 1–2 years		2–5 years		More than 5 years		Time unspecified[1]		Total	
Available for:	37/38	52/53	37/38	52/53	37/38	52/53	37/38	52/53	37/38	52/53
Full time work	6	6	2	5	3	3	1	5	12	19
Part time work	5	11	17	18	4	39	16	30	42	98
Total available	11	17	19	23	7	42	17	35	54	117
No wish to return to work									22	9
Did not reply									3	10

[1] These graduates said they would like to return to work at some time in the future, but could not foresee when this might be.

groups had last been in teaching, and wished to return to it, and a number said they would like to do social welfare work of some kind. Several of the graduates said they would only consider returning to paid employment if it were financially necessary, and that they would prefer to do voluntary social work of some kind. They felt that there was a need for trained women in voluntary work, which would suffer if too many returned to paid employment.

Table 63 shows how long ago the unoccupied graduates gave up paid employment, and what they were doing at the time. The 1937/1938 graduates who had been 16 or more years unemployed are those who have not worked since the end of the war. Most of these had no wish to return to work in the future.

It is clear that even among the younger graduates most of them had not worked for several years. Those who wished to return to work were asked whether they considered a refresher course of some kind would be useful; they were also asked for their views on the desirability of some form of television refresher courses.

Out of the 171 women of both age groups who wished to return to work, 130 welcomed the idea of refresher courses. Some of the subjects they wished to cover were general teaching, teaching handicapped children, medicine, social work, public health, domestic science, secretarial work and geographical research. They mostly preferred those courses which would bear some relation to their own subject, but some wished to break new ground, either to satisfy an ambition for fresh knowledge, or to follow a calling which would be more suitable to obtaining work in the district in which they were living.

TABLE 62. *Women now unoccupied: Type of Future Work envisaged, by Type of last job*

Type of future work		School-teaching	Universi-ties	Medicine	Industry	Govern-ment service	Other	No work since graduation	Total
Teaching	37/38	13	1	—	2	3	2	2	23
	52/53	38	10	—	5	4	12	2	71
Social work	37/38	1	—	—	—	4	3	—	8
	52/53	4	2	—	—	4	6	—	16
Medical	37/38	—	—	5	—	—	—	—	5
	52/53	2	—	7	—	—	—	—	9
Miscellaneous and no pre-ference	37/38	5	3	—	2	3	5	—	18
	52/53	2	3	—	6	1	13	2	27
No wish for work	37/38	5	2	1	—	4	5	5	22
	52/53	2	1	—	—	—	1	5	9

Most of the women said they would prefer refresher courses to be part time. Several had found great difficulty in obtaining refresher courses, since so many which are available involve full-time attendance, or short periods away from home, both usually difficult or impossible for the married woman. Almost all were of the opinion that far more refresher

TABLE 63. *Graduates now unemployed: Time since last Job, and type of last Job*

Time since last job	School-teaching	Universi-ties	Medicine	Industry	Civil service and local government	Other	Total
1937–1938 graduates							
1–5 years ago	9	3	2	—	1	4	19
6–15 years ago	10	1	2	4	4	5	26
16 years and over	4	2	2	2	8	8	26[1]
1952–1953 graduates							
1 year or less	13	7	1	—	—	10	31
2–3 years	15	6	2	3	3	8	37
4–5 years	11	1	3	3	4	9	31
6 years and over	9	2	—	7	2	7	27

[1] 7 graduates never worked since graduation. 1 did not answer the question.

courses should be available, particularly those aimed at the pre-war graduates who, after a long period at home, find it difficult to start work again. One suggestion was that corres-pondence courses combined with teaching in a local school as a student might prove useful. Another was that there should be paid refresher courses of up to six months for graduates between 30 and 50 years old who could make a useful contribution to teaching. The receipt of a salary would enable a married woman to make adequate provision for her family during the time of this intensive course.

Many of these graduates thought there should be more information available as to the type of job open to those wishing to return to work. Several commented on the difficulty of hearing of part-time work other than teaching; particularly outside London.

Out of the 130 women who would welcome a refresher course, only 38 thought television refresher courses would be useful. The remaining 92 thought they would be of little or no value. A number did not own, and did not wish to own television sets, and several graduates living overseas pointed out that there was still no television service in many countries. The other objections to television courses were that they would lack the personal contact between pupil and teacher which is desirable for a successful course, and that there would be no opportunity of meeting other students with similar problems, to ask questions or hold discussions.

The small number who saw possibilities in television refresher courses thought that they might prove valuable for some subjects, particularly scientific subjects, and would be useful for those living in remote districts where there is no possibility of local courses. They would take up the minimum amount of time, and would not necessitate making arrangements for looking after the children.

10. Refresher courses for those now in part-time work

Most of those in part-time work had no intention of returning to full-time work, and few had any interest in refresher courses. Most of those who were interested wished for some form of teacher-training course. A few, having done some teaching without taking a Diploma of Education, felt that they would like to attempt this, but were unable to attend a full-time course. A part-time course does not lead to a full diploma, and it was suggested that some compromise course might be instituted, in which the practical experience already gained could be taken into account.

11. Part-time work in general

Table 61 showed that most of the unoccupied graduates who envisaged returning to work wished to do so part time. Most of those who were working part time when they filled in the questionnaire had started their work after a period of unemployment. Their experience and opinions on the availability of part-time work are therefore of interest. What follows is a summary of the comments made by those graduates.

The choice of work for the married woman with children is largely regulated by the readiness of employers to accept women who have domestic responsibilities, and their willingness to adapt working conditions to the mutual benefit of employer and employee. The scope is often limited by the necessity of being more available at home during school holidays. Some of the women with an arts degree did not find it easy to find suitable work again, especially outside London or the larger cities, except in teaching or private coaching. Teaching certainly has the obvious advantages of being open to women willing to work part time and of providing holidays which coincide with those of the children. Most schools are prepared to make arrangements to suit the domestic ties of married women, and the value of the contribution of an older married woman, with children of her own, is becoming more generally recognised. It would seem from the comments of the graduates that private schools may offer more opportunities for part-time work, as they are often more flexible so far as hours are concerned. It was suggested that more married women would be encouraged to teach if an income tax allowance were made for domestic help in such circumstances. Several graduates considered that if part-time teaching were eligible for superannuation many more would be attracted back to the profession.

In universities and technical and training colleges there are a number of part-time posts available, but some of the graduates felt that there was a tendency for the responsibilities of married life to reflect somewhat adversely at times on their work, and that it was difficult to keep abreast of modern advances, particularly in scientific subjects. Refresher courses seem urgently required here. Work in some technical colleges has been found to be particularly suitable for married women, as hours are comparatively light, and there is opportunity for changing from full- to part-time work and vice versa.

The question of the married woman wishing to return to the medical profession after some years of devotion to domestic responsibility raised a number of problems. At present, part-time work seems somewhat difficult to find, especially perhaps in private practice, when it is difficult because of family responsibilities to take regular evening surgeries. There would seem, however, to be some scope for part-time work in private group practice, where hours would be more flexible, and in clinics and public health work. It was said that in medical teaching and research more part-time work should be made available, as at present there are few such posts to be found. This kind of medical work has been found to lend itself admirably to the particular circumstances of the married woman wishing to return to work, especially in fields in which there is comparatively little competition, and for which the married woman is particularly suited, such as pedriatrics and child psychiatry. There are also good prospects and much scope for part-time work in opthalmics.

An interesting point from one questionnaire was that in the United States a very large number of married women do full- or part-time work, and that some universities give 'Baby Sitting' Fellowships to enable married women to continue in pure research.

12. Other domestic responsibilities

We have so far discussed domestic responsibilities solely in terms of husband and children, but it should be remembered that many women, both single and married, may have additional responsibilities which may affect their ability and willingness to work. The care of elderly parents, or of sick dependants of any age can be both time-consuming and a financial liability. We asked the graduates if they had any responsibilities other than the normal care of husband and children. Table 64 shows the answers. Very few of the younger women had any other responsibilities, but more than a quarter of the older graduates answered 'yes' to this question; most of those in full-time work being single women. Few of these women said these responsibilities had any great effect on their working lives in determining the kind of work they did, or whether they worked or not, but for many of them their freedom to choose the area in which they worked was restricted.

TABLE 64. *Additional Domestic Responsibilities*

		United Kingdom			Overseas		
		Yes	No	Total	Yes	No	Total
Working full time	1937–38	21	59	80	3	6	9
	1952–53	7	73	80	—	23	23
Working part time	1937–38	11	30	41	—	1	1
	1952–53	2	35	37	—	8	8
Unoccupied	1937–38	20	42	62	1	16	17
	1952–53	6	104	110	1	25	26
Total	1937–38	52	131	183	4	23	27
	1952–53	15	212	227	1	56	57

13. The general availability of married women for work

It was clear that the majority of the unoccupied married women would like to undertake some paid work, but for many of them the possibility of working, particularly in a full-time job, depends almost entirely on the availability of reliable domestic help. Many of them were willing, even eager, to work when completely free of the ties of young children. A number contemplated working to help meet the cost of boarding school or university education. Some of them said that although willing to return to work, there was little financial incentive owing to their husband's tax liability, and the fact that the cost of domestic help has to be offset against any possible salary, with no allowances such as a business man can claim.

A point made by a number of the older women was that having young children to cope with in middle age, the question of taking an outside job is a matter of pure physical energy involved, and this is not available to everyone. Apart from the need of being more free during school holidays, the husband's work may affect the range of jobs available to the wife. The need to be free to move from one area to another may limit the chance of finding suitable part-time work. There was obviously a most willing potential labour force among these graduates, many of whom were anxious to widen their horizons beyond the home, and make more use of their university training, but it was also clear that many of them would feel unable to return to work unless they could more easily solve the problems of finding adequate domestic help and adequate refresher courses.

CHAPTER VIII

SUMMARY

1. Rate of response

(a) *The men.* 3748 men graduated in 1952 and 1953, of whom 594 could not be reached by post.

Of the remaining 3154, 2630 (83%) completed and returned the questionnaire. This represents a rate of response of 70% of the total number of graduates.

(b) *The women.* 613 women graduated in the years 1952, 1953, 1937 and 1938, of whom 59 could not be reached by post.

Of the remaining 554, 494 (90%) returned the questionnaire, representing a rate of response of 80% for the total number of graduates.

2. Background and qualifications (pages 6–15)

(a) *The men.* Their background was predominantly 'bourgeois', with parents belonging to the professional and managerial classes. Only 2% were the children of semi-skilled or unskilled workers.

Nearly two-thirds were educated at independent schools, just over a third at grammar schools (including direct grant schools).

Only 17% went straight to Cambridge from school. 66% were otherwise occupied for a period of one to three years. National Service was by far the commonest reason for the existence of this interval.

53% took degrees in arts subjects, 31% in science or mathematics, 11% in engineering.

9% achieved First Class Honours, 59% Second Class Honours, 26% Third Class Honours and 6% an Ordinary degree.

At the time of the survey the majority of the men were in the age group 29–33.

About a quarter were still bachelors, proportionally a little more than in the general population.

Two-thirds had acquired additional formal qualifications; certificates in education, medical or legal qualifications and Ph.D.s being the commonest.

Of the 2630 men who completed questionnaires all but 434 were working in the United Kingdom. 349 British nationals were working overseas. The remainder (53 Commonwealth and 32 foreign nationals) were working in their respective countries of origin.

(b) *The women.* Their home background was similar to the men, but relatively fewer were educated at independent schools. The majority went direct from school to Cambridge, where nearly two-thirds read for an arts degree, just over a third for a degree in science or mathematics.

The women gained relatively more Second Class Honours degrees and fewer Third Class Honours and Ordinary degrees than the men. The older group contained a significantly higher proportion of firsts than either the younger women or the men.

85

At the time of the survey the younger women were in the same broad age range as the men, but more were in the 29–31 age groups. The older women were in their forties.

72% of the younger and 63% of the older women were married. In both groups the proportion of single women was much higher than in the general population.

A fifth of each group held a Certificate in Education and about 8% were qualified in medicine.

Of the 494 women who completed questionnaires 227 of the younger women and 183 of the older women were British nationals living in the United Kingdom. 55 and 22 respectively were British nationals living overseas, and 2 and 5 respectively were foreign nationals living overseas.

3. Employment at the time of the survey

(a) *The women*

	1952–53	1937–38
Working full time	35%	43%
Working part time	16%	23%
Not working	49%	34%

Out of 207 married women 50 were working full time and 78 were working part time.

The most striking feature of the women's employment was the very high proportion of teachers in schools or universities. Only in medicine and the civil service, among other occupations, was the proportion of employed women as high as that of the men.

In Chapter VII the women's employment is discussed in more detail.

(b) *The men.* The men who were employed at the time of the survey were divided into *salaried employees*, *self-employed* and *men known to be employed in family businesses* (see Chapter III). The last class is really a sub-division of the first, but was kept separate because its members' earnings showed certain special characteristics.

The respective proportions in these categories for men in the United Kingdom were 84%, 13% and 3%.

The same proportions for men overseas were 92%, 5% and 3%.

Only 19 men (13 in the United Kingdom, 6 overseas) were unemployed: and 8 men in the United Kingdom were working part time.

Distribution of employment (pages 16–18)

The self-employed men were mainly in legal and medical practices, in agriculture or in commerce. A smaller number were practising as architects, accountants or advertising agents with a few free-lances in journalism, art and the entertainments business.

If all the men working in the United Kingdom are grouped together, industry and teaching are the most strongly represented occupations, each accounting for about 24% of the total.

About a quarter of the men in industry were engaged in research, design and development work and a similar number in sales and marketing. A little less than a fifth were in production management and a slightly smaller group in general management.

Three-fifths of the teachers were schoolmasters and two-fifths teaching in places of higher education.

Three-quarters of the schoolmasters were teaching arts subjects and only a quarter science, mathematics or engineering subjects. By contrast, in the universities and technical colleges men teaching the latter subjects outnumbered those teaching arts subjects in the ratio of 57:43.

Medicine and commerce claimed roughly an equal share of the whole group—each 8%.

6% were ministers of religion and 5% were practising lawyers.

9% were public servants in the Civil Service, local authorities or the Atomic Energy Authority. (4% in the Scientific Civil Service, 3% in professional or specialist classes, 2% in administration.)

No other employment group contained as many as 3% of the men, except agriculture which just reached this level.

Only 1% were in practice as accountants.

Type of work (page 19)

Table 16 in Chapter III shows the kind of work the men were doing in the various employment groups. Taking all the employment groups together, teaching was the most common occupation (23%), followed by research, design and development (13%), then by sales, advertising and marketing (9%), and general administration and management of various kinds (9%).

Degree subject and employment (page 23)

Nearly 60% of the *engineering* graduates were in industry with 27% divided about equally between firms of consultants and H.M. Forces. (A group of commissioned officers in all three fighting Services are sent to Cambridge each year to read mechanical sciences.)

Scientists and mathematicians were not so heavily represented in industry (41%), but were much stronger in universities and technical colleges (about 20%).

16% were teaching in schools, a proportion which falls far short of demand, but one which is not inconsiderable. It is nearly double the number employed in the Scientific Civil Service.

Teaching accounts for the largest single group of *arts graduates*. 23% were schoolmasters and, if those teaching in places of higher education are added, the figure rises to 30%.

A fifth of the arts men were in industry and about an eighth in commerce.

In industry about two-fifths of the arts men were in commercial departments and a quarter in general management or the central services of industrial groups. The rest were divided between production, accounting and personnel departments.

Degree class and employment (page 28)

More than a third of all the men with First Class Honours were in university posts. Industry and professional practices had about one in seven of them. The civil service had a large share in relation to the size of its entry.

The incidence of 2.i in professional practice was higher than in industry.

Only 3 schoolmasters in 100 had First Class Honours and only 2 of them had Ph.D.s. However, nearly a quarter had 2.i classes. But a surprisingly high proportion—nearly 10%—had Ordinary degrees.

Men with Ph.D.s were mainly in universities or in research appointments elsewhere. Few of them had taken doctorates in arts subjects.

4. Earnings and satisfaction (men working in the United Kingdom)

Earnings (page 30)

If the total earnings (i.e. salary plus the value of pension contributions and fringe benefits) of all the men are distributed, the middle members of the group were receiving between £1500 and £1600. If basic earnings (i.e. salary alone) are similarly treated, the median is at £1425.

A quarter had total earnings of less than £1250 and an almost equal number total earnings of over £2000. 12% were earning more than £2500.

The self-employed men, though their earnings were widely spread, did appreciably better than the salaried men.

The men employed in family businesses had even higher earnings. 58% were earning over £2500 as compared with 7% among the other salaried men. They were substantially better off than other men in industry and commerce. It must not be assumed, however, that this disparity will persist throughout their careers.

A third of the men in industry were earning over £2000, but nearly a quarter were earning less than £1500. The notion that industry is the lucrative occupation par excellence applies only to a small number of men in their early thirties.

Men in commerce and men in legal and other private practices tended to be a little better off than men in industry.

Medical men were earning less than lawyers and other professional practitioners.

The ministers of religion earned least (virtually all of them less than £1250).

Three-quarters of the schoolmasters fell into the group earning between £1000 and £1500. Only 3% were earning over £2000.

The university and technical college teachers did appreciably better than the schoolmasters, but only 7% earned more than £2000.

In two occupations—agriculture and journalism and entertainment—there was a large percentage with high and low earnings and relatively few near the average for the whole group.

Class and subject (page 37)

The relationship between degree class and earnings was vitally affected by the tendency for men with distinguished degrees to enter occupations, particularly education and research, in which remuneration is moderate and salaries tied to a hierarchy. For this reason the men with First Class Honours seldom earned salaries over £2500. But they were less likely to earn below £1250 and more likely to exceed £2000 than men with lower classes in their degrees.

Men with Third Class Honours or Ordinary degrees were more likely than the rest to be earning less than £1250. But they were quite as strongly represented as the rest in the groups earning over £2000.

Emoluments (page 38)

The average value of emoluments (i.e. employers pension contributions and fringe benefits) was about 10% of salary. For most men the employer's pension contribution was by far the largest item.

Men in educational posts and in private practices enjoyed the least advantages from emoluments, men in the Churches and H.M. Forces the greatest.

Men of this age in industry do not appear to have access to the fringe benefits popularly ascribed to business men. The proportion of men (22%) deriving more than 12% of their earnings from emoluments was lower than in most other employment groups. More men in commerce fell into this category.

Comparison of men and women (page 35)

The women of 1952/53 tended to earn less than the men, mainly because the majority of them were in education. Only 4% of the younger women working full time (3 women) were earning over £2000, as against 18% of the employed men. The spread of earnings of the 1937/38 women working full time was more like that of the men, with 19% earning over £2000. It has to be remembered that very few women were employed in industry, commerce, or professional practices other than medicine; within the fields of education and the Civil Service their earnings were comparable with those of the men.

Satisfaction (page 41)

(i) *With salary*. Teaching was the only occupation in which the men who considered their salary a fair return for their work were outnumbered by those who thought otherwise, but even so nearly half were satisfied.

About a third of those employed in universities, in medicine and in private practices were dissatisfied with their earnings: and about a quarter in industry.

The groups who were least critical of their salaries were the Civil Service, research establishments, H.M. Forces, commerce, and journalism and entertainment.

(ii) *With their work in general*. The differences between employment groups in this respect were not spectacular.

Schoolmasters and civil servants were least disposed to express strong dissatisfaction, but they were not much different from the rest in the proportion who said that they were highly satisfied. Men in the universities most frequently expressed profound satisfaction (about 30%).

In industry marked satisfaction was less common and marked dissatisfaction more frequent than in the other groups, but the differences were not substantial.

Men professing moderate satisfaction were in the neighbourhood of 60 % in all groups.

5. The past and the future (men working in the United Kingdom)

(*a*) *The post-graduate period* (page 45). A little more than half the men went directly into paid employment after graduation. Apart from 196 who did National Service, most of those who did not immediately start permanent employment took full-time courses of study, the commonest being the 1-year post-graduate diploma of education, the 3-year Ph.D. course, and courses in medicine.

(*b*) *Starting salaries* (page 48). Men who entered paid employment within six months of graduation (i.e. in 1952 and 1953) were mostly paid between £400–£600 p.a. At the outset schoolmasters' salaries compared favourably with those of other employment groups. The proportion of men who had starting salaries of £600 or over was highest in industry, commerce and teaching.

Four years after graduation the average salaries of men who had taken post-graduate courses of study were slightly lower than those of men who had started employment immediately after graduation. This suggests that, at this stage, experience on the job was more likely to gain higher financial rewards than qualifications requiring full-time study. The main reason for this is probably that the men with good academic qualifications tended to enter research and university teaching, with less chance of the higher salaries paid in commerce and in industrial management.

(*c*) *Changes of employment* (page 52). Only 3 men who went into the Church or the medical profession subsequently changed their profession.

58% of the men who went into other occupations changed their employers at least once between starting their first job and the time of the survey. They included 29% who left the employment group in which they started. 16% made radical changes involving a change not only of employment group, but also of occupation.

The relationship between changes of employment and earnings is complex and difficult to evaluate. Among the men who had stayed put, there were more earning high salaries than among those who changed. Again, with a sizable number of exceptions, the men who made the most frequent and the most radical changes were not as well off as those who were less disposed to change. But at this age the long-term effect of changes could not readily be assessed.

The changes between the various employment groups nearly balanced one another, and the overall distribution of the men among the main employment groups was very similar at the time of the survey and at the time of first employment.

(*d*) *The future* (page 57). About half the men expected to be with the same employer, or in the same business, in 5 years time, although nearly a quarter of the salaried employees were not prepared to commit themselves on this point.

There was some evidence that those who had already had some change of employer were more disposed to contemplate further moves. Men in Government service, education, the Church and medicine had a clearer idea of their future prospects than the men in other fields.

The increase in earnings expected in 5 years' time was relatively lower for schoolmasters, civil servants and ministers of religion than for men in other employment groups. The highest percentage increases were predicted by men in legal practices, commerce, and medicine.

6. Men working overseas (pages 60–66)

434 men were working overseas at the time of the survey. The larger groups were in the U.S.A. (60 men), Canada (58 men), and in various African territories (131 men). It is probable, but not certain, that at least half those in Canada, and a substantial proportion of those in the U.S.A., were permanently resident overseas.

19% of the men working overseas were in government service, the majority in Africa. 20% were concerned with education in schools, in Africa, Canada, other Commonwealth territories, and in the U.S.A. 7% were employed in universities, the greater number in the U.S.A., with a small number in Africa, Australia and Canada. 20% were in industry, and 13% in commerce, their geographical distribution being extremely wide.

Degree subject did not seem to be related to a tendency to work overseas. About 16% of all the men who completed questionnaires were overseas at the time of the survey. Looking at the subject groups separately, 18% of the arts graduates were overseas, 16% of the scientists and mathematicians, and 13% of the engineers.

There were 25 engineers or scientists in the U.S.A., and 20 in Canada. Of the 29 Ph.D.s in overseas territories, 17 were in the U.S.A., almost all in university posts.

Men with Ph.D.s were not more likely to be working overseas than men with other qualifications.

Earnings overseas appeared to be much higher than earnings in the United Kingdom, with a third of the men earning the equivalent of £3000 or over. However, differences in the cost of living in the overseas territories makes direct comparison impossible.

7. The women graduates (pages 67–84)

Their general background and qualifications are described in Chapter II. The following is a summary of the position at the time of the survey.

(i) *The 1952/1953 graduates*

(a) 36% of the 284 women of 1952/1953 were in full-time employment at the time of the survey. Rather more than two-thirds of these were single women; just under a third were married.

7% of the whole group—all married women—were in part-time employment of more than 10 hours a week. 9% were in part-time employment of 10 hours a week or less.

48% were not in paid employment at the time of the survey. All but 4 of these were married, most of them with young children.

(b) *The 1952/1953 graduates in paid employment.* 24% of the 148 women who were working, full or part-time, were teaching in schools; 20% were teaching in universities or technical colleges.

The only other occupation groups of any size were doctors (11%) and Government servants (10% in the Civil Service and local government posts.) Other occupations included editors, writers and translators, secretaries, almoners, biochemists, school matrons and museum archaeologists.

The basic earnings of all the 1952/1953 women working full time had a median value of £1080 (i.e. earnings excluding superannuation and fringe benefits).

Total earnings (i.e. salary plus additional emoluments) were distributed so that 61% of those working full time were earning between £1000 and £1500 .15% had total earnings of £1500 or over. Only three of these younger women were earning £2000 or over, all in the Civil Service. 24% had total earnings of under £1000.

Part-time earnings ranged from under £150 up to between £1000 and £1500, although there were only 2 women in the higher range.

The range of 'satisfaction scores' (see Chapter IV) showed that, compared with men, a lower proportion of the women had scores at the dissatisfied end of the scale, and a higher proportion were at the satisfied end of the scale. Few expressed dissatisfaction with their earnings.

(c) *The 1952/1953 graduates who were not in paid employment.* 136 of the younger women were not in paid employment at the time of the survey (48% of the whole group). 19 of these said they would like to return to full-time employment at some time in the future; 98 envisaged taking up part-time work eventually. The majority of them, however, felt that they would not be in a position to return to work for some years, and a number were unable to envisage any particular time. Most of these women have young children and were, understandably, unable to predict what their position might be by the time the children were old enough to make outside work a practicable possibility.

(ii) *The 1937/1938 graduates*

(a) 42% of the 210 1937/1938 women graduates were in full-time employment at the time of the survey; a quarter of them were married.

12% were in part-time employment of more than 10 hours a week; all but 2 of these were married or widowed. 8% were in part-time employment of less than 10 hours a week.

38% were not in paid employment at the time of the survey; only 2 of them were single.

(b) *The 1937/1938 graduates in paid employment.* 44% of those who were working, full or part time, were schoolteachers, a markedly higher proportion than the younger women. 13% were university teachers, 8% were doctors, and 11% were in government service. The remaining 24% were in a variety of different occupations.

The median basic earnings of the 1937/1938 women working full time was £1455. 38%

had total earnings of between £1000 and £1500; 25% of between £1500 and £2000, and 19% of £2000 or more. 5 of these women were earning £3000 or over, in medicine or the Civil Service. 18% had total earnings of less than £1000.

Part-time earnings were mainly below £500. 3 who were working part time were earning £1000 or more, in medicine or university teaching.

The range of satisfaction scores was similar to that of the younger women, but a slightly greater proportion had high scores. It would appear that the women as a whole were less prone to dissatisfaction with their work than the men.

(c) *The 1937/1938 graduates who were not in paid employment.* Out of the 79 older women who were not in paid employment, 54 said they would like to return to work. 12 of these thought they might do full-time work, and 42 expressed preference for part-time work. Only 11 envisaged returning to work within the next 2 years; 19 thought they would take up work within 5 years; 7 thought it was unlikely to be as soon as this, and 17 could not predict a particular time.

(iii) *Conditions for returning to work*

Many of the women of both age groups who envisaged an eventual return to paid employment did not express strong preferences for any particular kind of work; the most important consideration was simply that it should be interesting and useful. Most of those who expressed a preference specified school-teaching, and a number felt they would like to do social work of some kind. School-teaching combines the advantages of being a rewarding occupation, filling an urgent need, and being relatively adaptable to the demands of domestic responsibilities.

Pay was a secondary consideration with most of them, but several pointed out that it would need to be at least sufficient to cover the cost of domestic help, preferably with something over.

The majority of those wishing to return to work welcomed the idea of some kind of refresher course before doing so. The older women, in particular, stressed that this was essential after many years away from paid employment, not only in bringing their knowledge up-to-date, but also in increasing their confidence.

A number of the women, however, felt that existing refresher courses were too few, or insufficiently publicised, and that they too often entailed full-time attendance, away from home.

It was clear that although there were a number of women who would welcome the opportunity of taking up paid employment, many of them felt that this was unlikely to become a reality unless they could find adequate domestic help.

It is encouraging to note the wide range of essential services both sets of women graduates are performing, and the high proportion who are teaching both at school and at University levels. But for the domestic labour shortage many more would be in paid employment but even as things are, it is clear that the educational attainments of these women have by no means been wasted.

APPENDIX I

THE QUESTIONNAIRE

1. General scope of the enquiry

The terms of reference were wide, in terms of both time and subject matter, and suggested some lines of enquiry which, so far as we know, had not previously been followed in a postal survey (as distinct from personal interviews). Questions about status and satisfactions inevitably involved expressions of opinion and subjective judgments and presented problems of definition and analysis which needed careful thought. It is often held that postal surveys should deal only with factual information; Scott, however, in a comprehensive review of research on mail surveys concludes that 'on the existing published evidence, the mail survey does not appear to be necessarily any less efficient than the interview as a means of collecting information and opinions from the public, unless the questions or their interrelations are complex'.*

In planning a postal questionnaire to cover so wide a time-span and range of activities we had to accept the fact that, if it was not to be unduly long, we should almost certainly have to omit either some of the detail or some of the items of information we should have liked to ask for. There is little published evidence about the limitations on length of a successful mail survey,* and such as there is relates mainly to surveys of the general population, whereas we were dealing with a group which could be presumed to have some special interest in the enquiry. We therefore decided to subject the draft questionnaire to a fairly severe pilot test. Two successive versions were piloted for the men, and one for the women.

As a result of these trials, we concluded that we could not collect information which we could use as a meaningful measure of status and levels of responsibility, or which could afford a legitimate means of comparison between different categories of responsibility, but that questions on satisfactions produced answers which, while needing cautious interpretation, could be used to show general trends of opinion.

On the question of length, the pilot surveys suggested that Cambridge graduates would eventually respond well to a request from the University to fill in a rather long questionnaire, but that a fairly high proportion of them were unlikely to do this quickly, and that more than one reminder would be needed to obtain a high response rate.

2. The questionnaire

The final questionnaire was a rather formidable-looking document, consisting of 15 printed pages for the men, 13 for the women. However, no one was asked to fill in the whole of this. It was arranged so that there was a choice of 3 sections to be filled in, according to the graduate's current occupation. This increased the total bulk of the questionnaire, but meant that we could manage with fewer instructions and explanations than would have been needed with a single set of questions directed to everyone. The bulk of the questionnaire was also increased by using fairly large print and generous spacing; several of the pilot respondents had remarked on the advantages of this.

The subject matter of the questionnaire was of three kinds:†

* Scott, C., *Research on Mail Surveys*, J.R.S.S. Series A, 124, 1961.
† Owing to printing costs, the questionnaire is not reproduced in this report. Copies are available from the University Appointments Board, 6 Chaucer Road, Cambridge, but the number is limited, and we should be grateful if only those interested in the methodological aspect of the survey would apply.

94

(i) Factual questions about the graduate's background and experience. These covered his date of birth, marital status, parents occupation, schooling, university examinations and activities since graduation. He was asked to describe his current job and earnings in some detail and to give rather less detail about previous jobs and earnings.

(ii) Questions asking for descriptive details and comments on factual situations. The main purpose of these questions was to aid interpretation of the factual answers. To give an example: After questions about the graduate's employer, Question 6 in Section B asked 'What is your own job?' and asked the graduate to 'give the title or grade of the post and describe the nature of the work'. Those familiar with problems of occupational classification will realise that answers to this may range from a detailed account of a research project to a description which reads 'Engineer; nature of work, engineering'. As we wished to classify occupations in terms of the kind of work involved the latter description would not have been very helpful. Question 5 (asking for the name of the department in which the graduate worked) often gave the necessary information, but the pilot experience had made it plain that even so there might be many borderline cases. Question 8 asked for an assessment of the relative amount of time devoted to different functions, and this was extremely valuable in clarifying otherwise doubtful answers.

A further example of a question designed to aid interpretation is Question 13, which, having asked the graduate for the date of his first appointment after graduation, asked what he did in any gap between graduation and starting work, and then 'what, if any, bearing did this have on your subsequent career?' The resulting comments were not analysed as such, but were extremely useful in coding both the nature of the first appointment, and the nature of any preliminary activities.

(iii) Opinion questions, not basically factual, calling for subjective answers. The chief questions here are those on satisfactions with pay and general conditions and the questions dealing with the graduate's future. Here we were looking for trends of opinion. The answers to questions on future movements and earnings are not presented as glimpses into the future, but as an indication of how far the graduates felt settled in their current jobs, and how far they felt able to look ahead in their particular occupations.

3. Response

The questionnaire was sent out to the men in 5 separate dispatches in July and August 1961; to the women in a single dispatch in August. Reminders were sent out to the 6 different groups at slightly varying intervals of about 4–6 weeks. 4 reminders were sent to some groups, 3 to others. A duplicate questionnaire was sent with some of the third reminders. A pre-paid post-card was enclosed with the final reminder (whether third or fourth) asking the graduate to state his occupation, and to indicate whether or not he intended to return the questionnaire eventually. It was hoped by this means to gain some information from potential non-respondents in order to assess the possibility of non-response bias.

Addresses were obtained from college records. After a lapse of 8 or 9 years it was to be expected that a number of graduates should have lost touch with their colleges. The college records listed 3748 graduate men of 1952 and 1953, but had no address for 149 of these. Questionnaires were sent out to the remaining 3599 men. 433 of these were returned, address unknown, and 12 because the graduate had died. This left an effective sample of 3154 men.

Completed questionnaires were received from 2630 men, giving an effective response rate of 83%. 112 replied indicating their unwillingness or inability* to complete the questionnaire; 13

---

* This included 6 men who had been ill for some years, and had worked only intermittently or not at all since graduation.

replied stating that they would complete the questionnaire in due course but did not, in fact, do so. No reply was received from 400 men (17% of the original total of 3748).

The women responded better than the men. There were 613 graduates on the college lists for the years 1952 and 1953, 1937 and 1938, but no address for 31 of the women. 528 questionnaires were sent out, 28 returned, address unknown. 494 completed questionnaires were received, an effective response rate of 90% (80% of the 613 names on the college lists). 14 women replied saying they were unwilling to complete the questionnaire and there was no reply from 40 of them.

Since the questionnaire covered several aspects of the graduate's experience, it was inevitable that some respondents did not answer all the relevant questions, and we had to decide at what stage a questionnaire could be regarded as 'complete', and when it should be discarded as too incomplete for analysis and classified as a refusal. Since the main object of the survey was to discover what jobs the graduates were doing at the time of the survey, it was essential to have at least enough information to classify the graduate's current occupation, and to know what subjects he read when he was up at Cambridge. There were a few cases where the graduate gave us quite a lot of background information, but did not tell us about his current occupation, and these have been excluded from the analysis. There were also some who did not give us sufficient information about their current earnings. We eventually decided to include these with the completed questionnaires, provided there was enough other information to classify the employment group and type of work. There were 21 cases of this kind.

The number who gave no answer, or uncodeable answers to other questions was variable. Answers containing obvious inconsistencies, or whose meaning was very unclear, were coded as 'not known', together with the cases which gave no reply at all to a particular question.*

Because of the variation in the number who gave answers to different questions, the total numbers in the tables of results are not always the same. Where the number of unknowns was large and the possibility of bias appears important, we have commented in the appropriate place in the main report.

The general quality of the response was good, in so far as the majority of those who completed questionnaires had clearly given much time and thought to their answers; many went out of their way to annotate their answers so as to leave us in no doubt as to their meaning, and many made good use of the fairly generous scope for comment on various aspects of graduate experience. Even those (relatively few) who were daunted by the length of the questionnaire and who had no time or inclination to answer the opinion questions answered the factual questions with what appeared to be reasonable care. There is little doubt that the good quality of the response was due partly to the fact that this was a special group of the population, who could be assumed to have above average intelligence, and particularly to the fact that the survey was sponsored by the University. Several graduates said that they were quite willing to co-operate because it was a university enquiry, implying that they would have been much less willing to oblige any other body.

4. Reliability of the information

There are three sides to the question of reliability: (a) the accuracy of the answers used in the analyses, (b) the extent to which the responding sample can be considered representative of Cambridge graduates of 1952 and 1953, both overall and within particular sub-groups, (c) the extent to which graduates of those two years are representative of other generations of recent graduates.

---

* There were some questions where it was interesting to try to distinguish graduates who did not themselves know the answer from those whose answer was missing or incomprehensible, e.g. questions on future prospects and earnings.

96

(a) Accuracy. We have not checked the validity of the answers, and there are only a few items of information for which this could be done.† The results therefore show the graduate's own answers, and it is of course possible that there were some errors due to memory difficulties and rationalisation. Commonsense suggests that there must be differences in the accuracy with which the graduates were able to recall various situations, and one would expect answers about the immediate present to be more reliable than information about events occurring some years ago. Data on current earnings seems likely to be fairly accurate, and were usually in reasonable agreement with what is known about levels of pay in various occupations. Information about past salaries must be treated with more caution. A number of graduates could not remember their past salaries, or could only give figures for certain points in time. (See also Chapter V which presents the information about past earnings.) It must be assumed that many of those who did give values were giving approximate figures, and small differences between groups should not be given too much weight. However, there was sufficiently good agreement within occupation groups to make the figures worth presenting as a general indication of progress. (We were surprised at the number of graduates who had income tax returns or pay slips for some years back, and were able to give very precise figures in consequence.)

Information about other past events is less likely to be inaccurate; it is reasonably easy to remember what jobs you have held in the past eight years, even if it is not always easy to remember precisely what you were paid. The date at which events occurred may present some difficulties but we were more interested in the kind of changes that had taken place, less interested in when. There were some questions where it was important to know the date of some event; for example, the year in which the graduate came up to Cambridge and when he took his first appointment after graduating. There was, however, sufficient internal evidence in the questionnaire to give some check on consistency, and if there were obvious discrepancies, a 'don't know' answer was recorded.

The 'accuracy' of non-factual answers is more open to question, since it has to be remembered that there is room for variation in interpretation. The respondent's interpretation of the question may vary (and we do not claim that all the questions were unambiguous), so may the coder's interpretation of the answer. The chief disadvantage of a postal survey is the impossibility of explaining precisely what we think we mean by a question, and of prompting the respondent's reply if necessary. However, provided these limitations are borne in mind, there seems to be some value in embellishing a mainly factual account of what Cambridge graduates do with some general indications of what they feel about their work.

(b) How well does the responding sample represent all Cambridge graduates of 1952 and 1953? The first point to note is that we tried to include the whole population of Cambridge graduates of these two years. The respondents are a 'sample' only because some of the graduates could not be traced and others did not reply. The sample was therefore a self-selected one and, since it includes 70% of the population, the question of bias is obviously far more important than that of sampling error. A certain amount of information (on degree subject, class and age) about the non-respondents is available from the University records; this is presented overleaf. It shows a very little difference between the degrees taken by respondents and non-respondents (the latter are slightly biased towards arts subjects and the third class), but the non-respondents do seem to include a rather higher proportion of the older men. Thus the respondent sample appears to be biased, if at all, slightly towards those of the more 'typical' undergraduate age.

Unfortunately, we cannot compare the two groups in respect of any other characteristics. Although our final reminder asked everybody to send us information about occupation, we have

† We hope to include the results of some validity tests in a further article on some methodological aspects of the survey.

this for only 140 of the non-respondents. Their occupations are widely scattered and clearly give us no idea at all about the whole group of 1104 non-respondents. We cannot rule out, therefore, the possibility that non-response is far more important in some occupation groups than in others, or that it has led to bias in our findings for some of the other smaller sub-groups of the population. We can only say that there seems no reason to suspect any serious overall bias and that if it exists at all it is more likely to be among some of the smaller sub-groups which appear in some of the

	Respondents (percentage)	Non-respondents (percentage)
(i) Degree Class		
1	9	7
2.i.	19	18
2.ii.	30	29
2 undivided	10	9
3	26	31
Pass and Ordinary	6	6
Total men	2630	1104

	Respondents (percentage)	Non-respondents (percentage)
(ii) Subject		
Engineering	11	8
Natural Sciences I	12	13
Natural Sciences II	12	10
Mathematics	6	6
Economics	4	4
Law	13	15
Other arts	37	41
Agriculture, estate management and architecture	5	5
Total men	2630	1104

	Respondents (percentage)	Non-respondents (percentage)
(iii) Age		
33 or under	94	89
34–39	5	8
40 and over	1	2
Not known	—	1
Total men	2630	1104

analyses. We have, in any case, considered it worth while to present some of our findings in quite considerable detail, since this is the form in which it is most meaningful both to potential users of the information and to those who supplied it and may wish to compare themselves with their fellows.

(c) *How well do 1952 and 1953 graduates represent other recent generations?* It is in this context that our graduates of two years are to be thought of as a 'sample'; although, coming from two specified consecutive years, they are certainly not a truly random one. However, reasons have already been given (in Chapter I) for regarding 1952 and 1953 as reasonably 'normal' years; and it follows, if these arguments are accepted, that for many purposes the sample may be considered as broadly representative of recent generations of graduates. Clearly it is not representative in every respect. Some of its characteristics are known to have been changing with time over the past 10 years. For instance, the proportion of men reading science and engineering has increased slightly and the proportion reading arts subjects has dropped a little; the proportion of men from independent schools who come up without an award or scholarship is also declining; and with the abolition of National Service the average age of young Cambridge graduates is falling: but such changes are not great and, although they will have some effect on the total picture, are unlikely to have influenced the situation within occupational or subject groupings very much.

If we are regarding these graduates as a sample of all those of, say, the last 10–12 years, it becomes appropriate to ask how far our results may be affected by sampling error. Even a truly random sample may not be entirely representative of the population from which it was drawn, because it may happen, *by chance*, that it includes a number of extreme cases which are very rare in the population. The smaller the sample on which an estimate is based, the greater is the danger of this sort of error. The 'standard error' of a sample statistic gives an indication of the probability that the sample estimate differs from the true population value by more than a specified amount. Broadly speaking, in a random sample, there is only one chance in twenty that the true value differs from the estimate by more than double the standard error.

As we have said, our sample is not a random one; but it may nevertheless be helpful to the reader who wishes to generalise from it to give him some idea of the possible importance of sampling error. Many of our results are shown as percentages, and we therefore give below a table of the standard errors of various percentages in random samples of different sizes.

Standard error of a proportion

(in percentage points)

Proportion	Sample size					
	50	100	200	500	1000	2000
10% or 90%	4·3	3·0	2·1	1·4	0·9	0·7
25% or 75%	6·2	4·3	3·1	2·0	1·4	1·0
33% or 67%	6·7	4·7	3·4	2·1	1·5	1·1
50%	7·1	5·0	3·6	2·2	1·6	1·1

But by far the most important qualification which has to be made in thinking of these men and women as a typical group of graduates is that none of our financial results make any allowance for the changing value of money or for changes in the relative remuneration of different occupations. So far as our particular group of graduates is concerned, these changes are, in effect, already incorporated in our results. But earlier or later generations, for whom the changes have come at different points in their careers, may find that their financial progression has a rather different pattern. General salary movements are, for instance, notably stickier in some professions than in others; the pattern of salary progression in one of these occupations depends quite a lot on whether entry is just before or just after a general increase. Such difficulties cannot be avoided in a dynamic world; but they must be borne in mind in any attempt to project our story of past achievements into an assessment of future prospects.

DEGREE SUBJECT

The table below shows the distribution of subjects, discussed under subject headings in Chapter II.

Subject	1952/1953				1937/1938 Women	
	Men		Women			
	Number	Percentage	Number	Percentage	Number	Percentage
Engineering studies	42	2	—	—	—	—
Mechanical sciences I	165	6	1	—	—	—
Mechanical sciences II and chemical engineering	80	3	—	—	—	—
Natural sciences I	315	12	24	8·5	33	16
Natural sciences II	309	12	58	20·5	19	9
Mathematics II	97	4	20	2	24	11
Mathematics III	53	2	2	1	2	1
Law	333	13	6	2	4	2
Economics and social anthropology	92	4	12	4	7	3
Classics	104	4	18	6	19	9·5
English	115	5	31	10·5	19	9·5
Geography	89	3	24	8·5	11	5
History	290	11	24	8·5	27	13
Modern and medieval languages	178	7	34	12	26	12
Theology	98	4	5	2	1	0·5
Other arts	53	3	21	7·5	17	8
Agriculture	68	3	2	1	—	—
Estate management	40	1·5	—	—		
Architecture	24	0·5	2	1	1	0·5
Total	2545	100	284	100	210	100

1. Change of subjects

23% of the men changed their subject while studying for their degree. (The information has not been analysed for the women.)

3% of the men (76 graduates) changed after passing an examination in the subject classified as their 'degree subject'. Half of these were men who read natural sciences, part I, or mechanical sciences, part I, in their second year (both these being sufficient qualification for an Honours B.A.) and read another subject in their third year in order to fill in the necessary statutory residence required before the award of a degree. The remainder were arts graduates, most of whom had spent their first two years in reading one arts subject, passing part I of the tripos in their second year, and taking part I of another arts subject in their third year. In these cases the first subject was classified as their degree subject, as they had spent a longer time studying it.

507 men, 20%, changed their subject before taking the final examination classified as their degree subject. There was a small group of engineers who read natural sciences, part I, first and then changed to chemical engineering or mechanical sciences, part II, (30 men); and 10 scientists who had switched in the other direction, e.g. from mechanical sciences to physics. There were also 25 men who started reading mathematics, and went on to read physics.

Most of the changes were between arts subjects. The most common was a change from part I of an arts subject to part II in law. 211 men read law, part II, after some other subject; 67 after economics, 46 after history, 27 after modern languages, 21 after classics, 50 after the remaining arts subjects.

The other most common combinations were part I in English, classics or modern languages followed by part II in history, and classics or history, part I, followed by theology.

There were relatively few changes between arts and the sciences, mathematics and engineering groups. 32 who started by reading engineering, science or mathematics finished by reading law II, and 42 changed to other arts subjects. There were fewer changes in the other direction, only 15 men changing from an arts subject to science or mathematics.

2. Classification of main subject

If a graduate changed subjects before qualifying for his B.A., the 'main' subject was classified as follows:

Combination of subjects	Main subject classified
Part I of one subject followed by part II of another.	Part II subject.
Two part I subjects.	The part I subject which the graduate had studied for the longest period of time.
Two part II subjects.	The latest part II subject.

CURRENT EARNINGS OF MEN WITH ADDITIONAL POST-GRADUATE QUALIFICATIONS

The table below shows the total earnings of men with various post-graduate qualifications, irrespective of where they were working.

	Total annual earnings in 1961: £ per year[1]			Number of men
	Lower quartile	Median	Upper quartile	
Doctors	1380	1620	1860	194
Lawyers	1380	1850	2580	171
Accountants and actuaries	1500	1870	2400	78
Architects	1160	1440	1850	20
Estate management and surveyors	1280	1660	2190	31
Members of engineering institutions	1620	1870	2270	123
Diploma of Education	1050	1230	1430	222
Post-graduate diplomas and higher degrees requiring:				
1 year of study[2]	1380	1630	2330	30
2 years of study	1190	1450	1780	33
3 years of study	1350	1560	1820	159
Miscellaneous qualifications	1290	1660	2100	220
No post-graduate qualifications	1320	1690	2200	739

[1] Total earnings including additional emoluments. Median and quartile earnings shown in Chapter IV were basic earnings—i.e. excluding additional emoluments.

[2] Other than the post-graduate Diploma of Education and Church ordination.

For EU product safety concerns, contact us at Calle de José Abascal, 56–1°, 28003 Madrid, Spain or eugpsr@cambridge.org.

www.ingramcontent.com/pod-product-compliance
Ingram Content Group UK Ltd.
Pitfield, Milton Keynes, MK11 3LW, UK
UKHW030856150625
459647UK00021B/2786